Tapestry of Life

Biodiversity: A resource for secondary
teachers of English and Communication

Margaret Hubbard

Acknowledgements

The author and publishers thank all those who gave permission to reproduce copyright material (extracts and illustrations) in this publication. Acknowledgements are given beneath the relevant material within the text.

Every effort has been made to trace all the copyright holders but if any have been inadvertently overlooked the publishers will be pleased to make the necessary arrangements at the earliest opportunity.

First published 2001

© Learning and Teaching Scotland 2001

ISBN 1 85955 734 1

CONTENTS

INTRODUCTION

Biodiversity in English

This series of free-standing units has been devised to match the modes of Standard Grade English. A teacher could, for example, use just the material suggested for Talk, or for Discursive Writing. Alternatively, the units could be used across a number of modes to develop pupils' awareness of differing styles of language on the same theme.

What is biodiversity?

The word 'biodiversity' was first put together by an American scientist called Walter G. Rosen in 1985 for the 'National Forum on BioDiversity' in September 1986. The word is a combination of the Greek *bios,* meaning 'life', and 'diversity' meaning variety. Another American scientist, Edward O. Wilson, helped popularise the term in books such as *The Diversity of Life.*

In June 1992 representatives from the governments of over 150 countries met in Rio de Janeiro for a meeting called the United Nations Conference on Environment and Development (UNCED). What the governments discussed there was so important that the meeting came to be known as the 'Earth Summit'. Amongst many important documents that the world's governments adopted at that meeting was one called the 'Convention on Biological Diversity' – or the 'Biodiversity Convention' for short. This pledges governments to conserve biodiversity – to use its components in a way that will ensure that they continue to be available in the future and to share out the benefits of biodiversity fairly and equitably between all nations and all people. In all, 159 governments, including the United Kingdom as well as the European Union, signed the convention in Rio and it came into force in December 1993.

Put simply, 'biodiversity' means the total variety of all living things. Biodiversity is the *natural capital* that supports all our lives. It is vital for our survival and is a key measure of the health of our planet. Just as 'gross national product' measures the performance of the world's economic systems, biodiversity measures the performance of the world's life systems.

In the years since it was coined, the term 'biodiversity' has found its way into the policies of more than 150 countries around the world. The UK Government is one of the first in the world to be putting the concepts into practice. In Scotland the Scottish Biodiversity Group, an innovative partnership chaired by the Scottish Executive, is working on measures to protect and enhance biodiversity and to bring the concept to the heart of decision making both as an important process in its own right and as a key measure of success in achieving sustainable development.

What does biodiversity have to do with Standard Grade English?

The thinking for this publication emerged from an idea that, instead of environmental concerns being solely the province of school science departments, it might be possible to think about our world in other areas of the curriculum.

English is a very logical location for this topic because within English there is scope for discussion, reading and writing. English teachers are well aware that, as English is not content driven, any topic is valid for study.

Indeed the very relocation of environmental issues in English could itself be a catalyst to pupils' interest.

What does each free-standing unit contain?

Each unit contains work suitable for 200 minutes (five periods of 40 minutes). The work is constructed to suit mixed-ability or streamed S3/S4 classes. A teacher could therefore allocate one week to close reading using the passages provided (rather than past papers), or one week to discussion skills.

Another approach to the material would be to spend two weeks on biodiversity: one on close reading, one on talk. This would allow the students to explore a further dimension: the distinction between written and spoken language. A third approach would be to work on a section of each unit after reading a novel on a related topic, for example *The Day of The Triffids*.

The creative permutations of how to use this work should be decided by the teacher according to the needs of the class. The work is simply a resource the teacher can draw on, where previously no such resource on the topic of biodiversity existed.

It would be misreading this publication to perceive it as a return to 1970s-style thematic units. These tended to deal with issues, rather than the language in which the issues were explored. This package is an attempt to study the environment through studying the language. A thematic approach would need to bear this in mind.

THEMATIC APPROACH

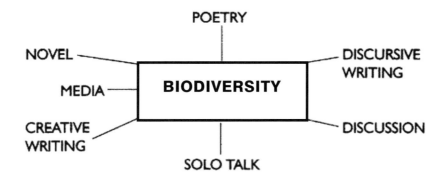

Should the teacher decide to tackle the theme of biodiversity, and hang all the work on it, all the units in this publication would make this possible. The material includes:
- discussion work
- Writing 1 and Writing 2 (non-fiction and imaginative)
- close reading
- CELs (critical evaluations of literature).

The work would be best approached in the order in which it appears so that each piece builds steadily on the previous piece of work.

The whole series of units begins with excerpts from Rachel Carson's *Silent Spring* published in 1963. It should end with pupils using one of the elements they have worked on, such as:
- discursive writing
- poetry
- media
- creative writing
- novel
- discussion
- solo talk

to develop their thoughts for the new century.

Teachers' introduction

The following excerpts from *Silent Spring* introduce the idea of biodiversity, and enable teachers and students to familiarise themselves with the concept.

It is essential to deal with this prologue as an introduction to the whole topic, as it provides a context for pupils not familiar with the debate.

Credit pupils should be able to handle the excerpts, while for General and Foundation pupils this introductory section will require paraphrasing. The simpler paragraphs have been identified by the use of an asterisk (*).

Alternatively, the excerpts could be used as a listening exercise.

In 1963 Rachel Carson published *Silent Spring*, in which she made an explicit link between the use of chemical pesticides and fertilisers and damage to plants and animals. While many people had already become concerned about the environment, the book acted as a catalyst and alerted a vast number of people to the environmental disaster that lay ahead if the human race did not alter its course. The ideas Rachel Carson expressed are still central to biodiversity and provide a well written, time-tested example of writing on the subject.

The passage below comes from an early chapter of the book and serves as an introduction to the environmental concerns in the units that follow.

Silent Spring

THE OBLIGATION TO ENDURE

THE HISTORY of life on earth has been a history of interaction between living things and their surroundings. To a large extent, the physical form and the habits of the earth's vegetation and its animal life have been moulded by the environment. Considering the whole span of earthly time, the opposite effect, in which life actually modifies its surroundings, has been relatively slight. Only within the moment of time represented by the present century has one species – man – acquired significant power to alter the nature of his world.

During the past quarter-century this power has not only increased to one of disturbing magnitude but it has changed in character. The most alarming of all man's assaults upon the environment is the contamination of air, earth, rivers, and sea with dangerous and even lethal materials. This pollution is for the most part irrecoverable; the chain of evil it initiates not only in the world that must support life but in living tissues is for the most part irreversible. In this now universal contamination of the environment, chemicals are the sinister and little-recognized partners of radiation in changing the very nature of the world – the very nature of its life. Strontium 90, released through nuclear explosions into the air, comes to earth in rain or drifts down as fallout, lodges in soil, enters into the grass or corn or wheat grown there, and in time takes up its abode in the bones of a human being, there to remain until his death. Similarly, chemicals sprayed on croplands or forests or gardens lie long in soil, entering into living organisms, passing from one to another in a chain of poisoning and death. Or they pass mysteriously by underground streams until they emerge and, through the alchemy of air and sunlight, combine into new forms that kill vegetation, sicken cattle, and work unknown harm

Silent Spring (continued)

on those who drink from once-pure wells. As Albert Schweitzer has said, 'Man can hardly even recognise the devils of his own creation.'

It took hundreds of millions of years to produce the life that now inhabits the earth – aeons of time in which that developing and evolving and diversifying life reached a state of adjustment and balance with its surroundings. The environment, rigorously shaping and directing the life it supported, contained elements that were hostile as well as supporting. Certain rocks gave out dangerous radiation; even within the light of the sun, from which all life draws its energy, there were short-wave radiations with power to injure. Given time – time not in years but in millennia – life adjusts, and a balance has been reached. For time is the essential ingredient; but in the modern world there is no time. The rapidity of change and the speed with which new situations are created follow the impetuous and heedless pace of man rather than the deliberate pace of nature. Radiation is no longer merely the background radiation of rocks, the bombardment of cosmic rays, the ultra-violet of the sun that have existed before there was any life on earth; radiation is now the unnatural creation of man's tampering with the atom. The chemicals to which life is asked to make its adjustment are no longer merely the calcium and silica and copper and all the rest of the minerals washed out of the rocks and carried in rivers to the sea; they are the synthetic creations of man's inventive mind, brewed in his laboratories, and having no counterparts in nature.

To adjust to these chemicals would require time on the scale that is nature's; it would require not merely the years of man's life but the life of generations. And even this, were it by some miracle possible, would be futile, for the new chemicals come from our laboratories in an endless stream; almost five hundred annually find their way into actual use in the United States alone. The figure is staggering and its implications are not easily grasped – five hundred new chemicals to which the bodies of men and animals are required somehow to adapt each year, chemicals totally outside the limits of biological experience.

Among them are many that are used in man's war against nature. Since the mid 1940s over two hundred basic chemicals have been created for use in killing insects, weeds, rodents, and other organisms described in the modern vernacular as 'pests'; and they are sold under several thousand different brand names.

These sprays, dusts and aerosols are now applied almost universally

Silent Spring (continued)

to farms, gardens, forests and homes – non-selective chemicals that have the power to kill every insect, the 'good' and the 'bad', to still the song of birds and the leaping of fish in the stream, to coat the leaves with a deadly film, and to linger on in soil – all this though the intended target may be only a few weeds or insects. Can anyone believe it is possible to lay down such a barrage of poisons on the surface of the earth without making it unfit for all life? They should not be called 'insecticides', but 'biocides'.

Rachel Carson, *Silent Spring*, Crest Books, 1963

Almost half a century ago, Rachel Carson saw that the whole tapestry of life was in danger of being destroyed forever, and that the result of this would have as yet unknown consequences.

The ideas introduced to many people in *Silent Spring* led directly to the Earth Summit in Rio de Janeiro in 1992 and to the world governments' pledge to take urgent action to secure the future of the Earth's resources. Out of this summit came the widespread use of the word 'biodiversity', from 'biological' and 'diversity', the rich variety of life. As a word it has predecessors: nature and environment. Biodiversity contains the essence of these words and makes explicit in its etymology that it is not just trees or birds or dolphins. It covers the whole living planet and the idea of interdependency of all species – including humans.

The Scottish Biodiversity Group was set up in 1996 to oversee action in Scotland as part of a coordinated UK strategy. It brings together not only government, its agencies, the local authorities, and voluntary environmental bodies, but also groups and organisations across a whole range of Scottish society, each with an important and distinctive part to play: farmers, fishermen, landowners, crofters, foresters, industrialists, researchers and scientists.

As civilians of the world we are all involved in the environmental debate, and each one of us has a part to play in respecting the Earth.

The introduction to *Silent Spring* by the explorer Sir Ernest Henry Shackleton allows none of us to shirk our responsibility.

Silent Spring (continued)

INTRODUCTION

IN THIS BRILLIANT and controversial book, Miss Rachel Carson brings her training as a biologist and her skill as a writer to bear with great force on a significant and even sinister aspect of man's technological progress. This is the story of the use of toxic chemicals in the countryside and of the widespread destruction of wildlife in America (caused by pesticides, fungicides and herbicides). But *Silent Spring* is not merely about poisons; it is about ecology or the relation of plants and animals to their environment and to one another. Ecologists are more and more coming to recognise that for this purpose man is an animal and indeed the most important of all animals and that however artificial his dwelling, he cannot with impunity allow the natural environment of living things from which he has so recently emerged to be destroyed. Fundamentally, therefore, Miss Carson makes a well-reasoned and persuasive case for human beings to learn to appreciate the fact that they are part of the entire living world inhabiting this planet, and that they must understand its conditions of existence and so behave that these conditions are not violated.

*We in Britain have not yet been exposed to the same intensity of attack as in America, but here too there is a grim side to the story. There have been, for example, the reports of a mysterious illness affecting foxes. The first substantial records of the 'fox death' were in November 1959 from near Oundle, in Northamptonshire, and soon reports were coming in from all over the country until it was estimated that 1,300 foxes had been found dead. There was much speculation as to the cause. It was suggested that death was due to a virus disease. The symptoms were striking. Foxes appeared dazed, partially blind, hypersensitive to noise, almost dying of thirst, and then death came. One odd symptom, as the Nature Conservancy reported, was that sick foxes appeared to lose their fear of mankind and were even to be found in such unlikely localities as the yard belonging to the Master of the Heythrop Hunt. No simple tests could at the time reveal the answer, but on the basis of more searching methods recently developed, 'fox death' is now generally believed to have been caused by the chlorinated hydrocarbons and other poisons so freely used in the countryside.

It was, however, the heaps of dead birds which revealed the truth. For many years biologists had given warning of danger, and already in

Silent Spring (continued)

1960 voices were raised in Parliament and elsewhere demanding restriction and even a ban on chemicals such as dieldrin, aldrin, and heptachlor. It was clear that control over their use was quite inadequate and appeals were made by official bodies for more care. Then came the spring of 1961, when tens of thousands of birds were found littering the countryside, dead or dying in agony. The story from one estate alone reveals the nature of the tragedy. In the spring of 1960 at Tumby in Lincolnshire heavy losses of birds were reported. In 1961 over 6,000 dead birds were counted. From the royal estate at Sandringham in Norfolk the list of dead birds included pheasants, red-legged partridges, partridges, woodpigeons and stock doves, greenfinches, chaffinches, blackbirds, song thrushes, skylarks, moorhens, bramblings, tree sparrows, house sparrows, jays, yellowhammers, hedge sparrows, carrion crows, hooded crows, goldfinches, and sparrowhawks. Over 142 bodies were collected in 11° hours of special survey counts, and hundreds more over a period of weeks. Amongst these birds were some, such as the bramblings, which are specially protected by law, yet all went down before the indiscriminate scythe of toxic chemicals.

Following this catastrophe, further pressure was brought to bear. The matter was urgently debated in Parliament. The Ministry of Agriculture, Fisheries and Food called meetings, the Nature Conservancy, backed by naturalist societies such as the Royal Society for the Protection of Birds, the British Trust for Ornithology and the Game Research Association intervened and finally a voluntary agreement was made to refrain from using certain seed dressings, except when an attack of wheat bulb fly was seriously anticipated, and then only for autumn sowings. But there is evidence that the poisoning from sprays still goes on, though undoubtedly the voluntary ban has led to a marked reduction in the number of bird deaths caused by toxic seed dressings. Sowing conditions were particularly favourable in 1961–62 which must have had an effect in reducing the casualty figures, yet many deaths were reported from widely separated places. Once again the death toll was heavy at Tumby, especially of pheasants where the fertility of the surviving birds was seriously affected. Nest desertions began earlier in the year and out of a sample of 740 pheasants' eggs, the number hatched was well below the normal and many of the chicks were small and soon died. With the [eggs which were shown to be infertile], there were present mercury and BHC (benzene hexachloride), both widely used as agricultural chemicals.

Silent Spring (continued)

The story of the peregrine is particularly significant. It is typical of the change in our countryside which is being wrought by toxic chemicals. The peregrine, with other predators, has an important role to play in the ecology of the countryside. If you look at a map of the distribution of the peregrine in 1962 you will see that it has largely disappeared from the south of England. In the north of England peregrines are still present in fair numbers but although some pairs laid eggs, more than half of these failed. The position is similar in southern Scotland. Only in the highlands and islands has there been a fairly normal nesting season. Investigation of an egg taken from an abandoned nest near Perth showed that here again was poison.

*Other predators, such as owls, have also been found dead. A significant example was that of a tawny owl from Kensington found dead on 9 July 1962. The bird was analysed by the Royal Society for the Protection of Birds' chemist and it was found to contain mercury, benzene hexachloride, heptachlor, and dieldrin. The tawny owl may well have been contaminated from eating rodents or insects in the gardens of London. A song thrush was also found dead in central London in the summer of 1962 with similar compounds in it. The number of garden chemicals on sale based on chlorinated hydrocarbons which are labelled 'safe' is a new and worrying factor, especially when one realises that some of these contain chemicals similar to those that have wrought such havoc in the fields. It is possible that even our gardens are becoming extremely dangerous places for wildlife.

In this country there have been no great government agencies spraying whole counties and States as in America against the fire ant, the spruce bud worm or the gipsy moth and in the process seriously damaging not only wildlife but even killing domestic animals. The nearest we came to it was in the 1950s when commercial interests tried to persuade British highway authorities to switch over to the widespread use of herbicide sprays on roadside verges and hedgerows. The horrible consequence of this is well described from American experience by Rachel Carson, but in this country the Nature Conservancy, backed by enraged naturalists, managed to insist on a standstill, except for experimental treatments. Both scientific tests and cost analysis showed that inflated claims and unsubstantiated requirements for mass chemicals would not stand up to examination and, therefore, the British wayfarer and taxpayer has been spared the outrages recorded in *Silent Spring*, although strictly limited spraying on main roads here is now permitted.

Silent Spring (continued)

*The human side is perhaps the most sinister part of this book and here I must leave it to Miss Carson to tell her own very thorough story. The fact is that chemical residues are to be found in the food we eat. We are told officially that there is no hazard but we are also told by Professor Boyland, of the Chester Beatty Institute, that there is no safe dose for a carcinogen and, if there were, we would not know what it was. We are eating these chemicals, possibly in small, possibly in large quantities, and certainly they are being stored in our livers and our fat. Whether or not the evidence contained in Miss Carson's fully documented story is accepted, the fact remains that until a thing can be shown to be positively safe, we ought to reckon that any contaminant should be avoided. No one would suggest spraying fields with radioactivity, yet we do not pause before using mutagenic chemicals, the effects of which have in certain respects been shown by Dr Alexander, also of the Chester Beatty Institute, to be the same. This is no simple matter, for there are already many chemicals added to our food and there are some contaminants that occur in nature which can be dangerous to human beings.

It would be unfair to suggest that there is complete indifference in official quarters in Britain. Bodies like the British Industrial Biological Research Association have been recently set up and are actively concerned with this problem. There are high-powered government and scientific committees and the Ministry of Agriculture, Fisheries and Food, however bland its public face, now exercises effective control to prevent the poisoning of agricultural workers and is doing a good deal more work in other parts of the field than it is generally given credit for. The same is true also of the chemical companies.

While we need to look at both sides of the coin, to remember such disasters as the Irish potato famine, yet there is a feeling of lack of urgency about the dangers, especially the hidden ones, in the use of certain poisons. The agricultural Establishment is so convinced of the great benefit in increased production through the use of these chemicals that when they come to balance the problem in utilitarian terms, they find it difficult to see the wider and longer-term consequences. It looks as if we will go on swallowing these chemicals whether we like it or not and their real effect may not be seen for another 20 or 30 years.

Nor is anything like enough research being done. This was clearly revealed in the report of the Sanders Committee. Are the gains to mankind such that we should continue to take a risk which admittedly

Silent Spring (continued)

many experts, but certainly not all, regard as negligible and, if so, are we prepared to ignore the destruction of wildlife and the cruelty? Here there is another danger and one that the ecologist is particularly aware of. Some years ago a serious plague attacked the cocoa crops in West Africa. It was found that the disease was caused by a virus found in a coccid protected by ants. The counter-attack was made on the ants, and the disease was reduced; but the natural balance was upset and later there was an outbreak of no less than four new insect plagues! Another chlorinated hydrocarbon, DDT, is already proving consistently less effective. There are no less than 26 kinds of malaria-carrying anopheles mosquito which are DDT-proof and the chemical weapons may prove to have broken in our hands.

The science of ecology teaches us that we have to understand the interaction of all living things in the environment in which we live. Fortunately in Great Britain there is an official agency, the Nature Conservancy, which exists to study the natural environment and to learn from research and experiment how to manage it and safeguard it so that there can be a harmonious coexistence between man and nature. Many people, however, look on the Conservancy as simply a body concerned with protecting birds, butterflies and wild flowers. It is urgently necessary that public opinion should understand more of the very serious and threatening problems with which such a body as the Conservancy has to deal, and *Silent Spring* will be an important means of enabling non-scientists to do so.

*The soil is not an inert thing; it is full of minute living creatures and plants on which we depend. Yet we spray poison wholesale over it. The death of the predators is a warning to perhaps the greatest predator of all – mankind. Recently at the Wildlife Fund dinner in London, Prince Bernhard of the Netherlands said:

We are dreaming of conquering space. We are already preparing the conquest of the Moon. But if we are going to treat other planets as we are treating our own, we had better leave the Moon, Mars and Venus strictly alone!

We are poisoning the air over our cities; we are poisoning the rivers and the seas; we are poisoning the soil itself. Some of this may be inevitable. But if we don't get together in a real and mighty effort to stop these attacks upon Mother Earth, wherever possible, we may find ourselves one day – one day soon, maybe – in a world that will be only a desert full of

Silent Spring (continued)

plastic, concrete and electronic robots. In that world there will be no more 'nature'; in that world man and a few domestic animals will be the only living creatures.

And yet, man cannot live without some measure of contact with nature. It is essential to his happiness.

I would ask those who find parts of this book not to their taste or consider that they can refute some of the arguments to see the picture as a whole. We are dealing with dangerous things and it may be too late to wait for positive evidence of danger. The tragedies of Thalidomide, of lung cancer from smoking, and many other examples, all these are a measure of the failure to foresee the risk and act quickly enough. A distinguished British ecologist said to me that he thought *Silent Spring* overstated some things now but in ten years' time or less these could be understatements.

Ideally, we should seek more profound solutions – resistant crop strains which would be a slow business to develop and, above all, ecological management to promote a natural balance which will also suit the needs of man. At present the university training in these fields is slight. This is not a soft option for the scientist nor, therefore, for mankind but it is one which we must face. It means more funds for fundamental research and perhaps less for developing new things directly for the market. The wildlife tragedy in the countryside involves ethical and aesthetic values and may bear on man's very survival. As the Duke of Edinburgh said at the Wildlife Fund dinner:

*Miners use canaries to warn them of deadly gases. It might not be a bad idea if we took the same warning from the dead birds in our countryside.

SHACKLETON
House of Lords, London.

Introduction to Rachel Carson, *Silent Spring*, Crest Books, 1963

Silent Spring (continued)

Finally, an explanation of the title of the book is made clear in a passage from Chapter 8.

AND NO BIRDS SING

OVER INCREASINGLY large areas of the United States, spring now comes unheralded by the return of the birds, and the early mornings are strangely silent where once they were filled with the beauty of bird song. This sudden silencing of the song of birds, this obliteration of the colour and beauty and interest they lend to our world have come about swiftly, insidiously, and unnoticed by those whose communities are as yet unaffected.

From the town of Hinsdale, Illinois, a housewife wrote in despair to one of the world's leading ornithologists, Robert Cushman Murphy, Curator Emeritus of Birds at the American Museum of Natural History.

Here in our village the elm trees have been sprayed for several years (she wrote in 1958). When we moved here six years ago, there was a wealth of bird life; I put up a feeder and had a steady stream of cardinals, chickadees, downies and nuthatches all winter, and the cardinals and chickadees brought their young ones in the summer.

After several years of DDT spray, the town is almost devoid of robins and starlings; chickadees have not been on my shelf for two years, and this year the cardinals are gone too; the nesting population in the neighbourhood seems to consist of one dove pair and perhaps one catbird family.

It is hard to explain to the children that the birds have been killed off, when they have learned in school that a Federal law protects the birds from killing or capture. 'Will they ever come back?' they ask, and I do not have the answer. The elms are still dying, and so are the birds. Is anything being done? Can anything be done? Can I do anything?

A year after the federal government had launched a massive spraying programme against the fire ant, an Alabama woman wrote:

Our place has been a veritable bird sanctuary for over half a century. Last July we all remarked, 'There are more birds than ever.' Then, suddenly, in the second week of August, they all disappeared. I was accustomed to rising early to care for my favourite mare that had a

Silent Spring (continued)

young filly. There was not a sound of the song of a bird. It was eerie, terrifying. What was a man doing to our perfect and beautiful world? Finally, five months later a blue jay appeared and a wren.

The autumn months to which she referred brought other sombre reports from the deep South, where in Mississippi, Louisiana, and Alabama the Field Notes published quarterly by the National Audubon Society and the United States Fish and Wildlife Service noted the striking phenomenon of 'blank spots weirdly empty of virtually all bird life'. The Field Notes are a compilation of the reports of seasoned observers who have spent many years afield in their particular areas and have unparalleled knowledge of the normal bird life of the region. One such observer reported that in driving about southern Mississippi that autumn she saw 'no land birds at all for long distances'.

Another in Baton Rouge reported that the contents of her feeders had lain untouched 'for weeks on end', while fruiting shrubs in her yard, that ordinarily would be stripped clean by that time, still were laden with berries. Still another reported that his picture window, 'which often used to frame a scene splashed with the red of forty or fifty cardinals and crowded with other species, seldom permitted a view of as many as a bird or two at a time.' Professor Maurice Brooks of the University of West Virginia, an authority on the birds of the Appalachian region, reported that the West Virginia bird population had undergone 'an incredible reduction'.

One story might serve as the tragic symbol of the fate of the birds – a fate that has already overtaken some species, and that threatens all. It is the story of the robin, the bird known to everyone. To millions of Americans, the season's first robin means that the grip of winter is broken. Its coming is an event reported in newspapers and told eagerly at the breakfast table. And as the number of migrants grows and the first mists of green appear in the woodlands, thousands of people listen for the first dawn chorus of the robins throbbing in the early morning light. But now all is changed, and not even the return of the birds may be taken for granted.

The survival of the robin, and indeed of many other species as well, seems fatefully linked with the American elm, a tree that is part of the history of thousands of towns from the Atlantic to the Rockies, gracing their streets and their village squares and college campuses with

Silent Spring (continued)

majestic archways of green. Now the elms are stricken with a disease that afflicts them throughout their range, a disease so serious that many experts believe all efforts to save the elms will in the end be futile. It would be tragic to lose the elms, but it would be doubly tragic if, in vain efforts to save them, we plunge vast segments of our bird populations into the night of extinction. Yet this is precisely what is threatened.

The so-called Dutch elm disease entered the United States from Europe about 1930 in elm burl logs imported for the veneer industry. It is a fungus disease; the organism invades the water-conducting vessels of the tree, spreads by spores carried in the flow of sap, and by its poisonous secretions as well as by mechanical clogging causes the branches to wilt and the tree to die. The disease is spread from diseased to healthy trees by elm bark beetles. The galleries which the insects have tunnelled out under the bark of dead trees become contaminated with spores of the invading fungus, and the spores adhere to the insect body and are carried wherever the beetle flies. Efforts to control the fungus disease of the elms have been directed largely towards control of the carrier insect. In community after community, especially throughout the strongholds of the American elm, the Midwest and New England, intensive spraying has become a routine procedure.

What this spraying could mean to bird life, and especially to the robin, was first made clear by the work of two ornithologists at Michigan State University, Professor George Wallace and one of his graduate students, John Mehner. When Mr Mehner began work for the doctorate in 1954, he chose a research project that had to do with robin populations. This was quite by chance, for at that time no one suspected that the robins were in danger. But even as he undertook the work, events occurred that were to change its character and indeed to deprive him of his material.

Spraying for Dutch elm disease began in a small way on the university campus in 1954. The following year the city of East Lansing (where the university is located) joined in, spraying on the campus was expanded, and, with local programmes for gypsy moth and mosquito control also under way, the rain of chemicals increased to a downpour.

During 1954, the year of the first light spraying, all seemed well. The following spring the migrating robins began to return to the campus as

Silent Spring (continued)

usual. Like the bluebells in Tomlinson's haunting essay 'The Lost Wood', they were 'expecting no evil' as they reoccupied their familiar territories. But soon it became evident that something was wrong. Dead and dying robins began to appear on the campus. Few birds were seen in their normal foraging activities or assembling in their usual roosts. Few nests were built; few young appeared. The pattern was repeated with monotonous regularity in succeeding springs. The sprayed area had become a lethal trap in which each wave of migrating robins would be eliminated in about a week. Then new arrivals would come in, only to add to the numbers of doomed birds seen on the campus in the agonized tremors that precede death.

'The campus is serving as a graveyard for most of the robins that attempt to take up residence in the spring,' said Dr Wallace. But why? At first he suspected some disease of the nervous system, but soon it became evident that

> in spite of the assurances of the insecticide people that their sprays were 'harmless to birds' the robins were really dying of insecticidal poisoning; they exhibited the well-known symptoms of loss of balance, followed by tremors, convulsions, and death.

Several facts suggested that the robins were being poisoned, not so much by direct contact with the insecticides as indirectly, by eating earthworms. Campus earthworms had been fed inadvertently to crayfish in a research project and all the crayfish had promptly died. A snake kept in a laboratory cage had gone into violent tremors after being fed such worms. And earthworms are the principal food of robins in the spring.

A key piece in the jigsaw puzzle of the doomed robins was soon to be supplied by Dr Roy Barker of the Illinois Natural History Survey at Urbana. Dr Barker's work, published in 1958, traced the intricate cycle of events by which the robins' fate is linked to the elm trees by way of the earthworms. The trees are sprayed in the spring (usually at the rate of two to six pounds of DDT per 50-foot tree, which may be the equivalent of as much as 23 pounds per acre where elms are numerous) and often again in July, at about half this concentration. Powerful sprayers direct a stream of poison to all parts of the tallest trees, killing directly not only the target organism, the bark beetle, but other insects, including pollinating species and predatory spiders and beetles. The poison forms a tenacious film over the leaves and bark. Rains do not wash it away. In the autumn the leaves fall to the

Silent Spring (continued)

ground, accumulate in sodden layers, and begin the slow process of becoming one with the soil. In this they are aided by the toil of the earthworms, who feed in the leaf litter, for elm leaves are among their favourite foods. In feeding on the leaves the worms always swallow the insecticide, accumulating and concentrating it in their bodies. Dr Barker found deposits of DDT throughout the digestive tracts of the worms, their blood vessels, nerves, and body wall. Undoubtedly some of the earthworms themselves succumb, but others survive to become 'biological magnifiers' of the poison. In the spring the robins return to provide another link in the cycle. As few as eleven large earthworms can transfer a lethal dose of DDT to a robin. And eleven worms form a small part of a day's rations to a bird that eats ten to twelve earthworms in as many minutes.

Not all robins receive a lethal dose, but another consequence may lead to the extinction of their kind as surely as fatal poisoning. The shadow of sterility lies over all the bird studies and indeed lengthens to include all living things within its potential range. There are now only two or three dozen robins to be found each spring on the entire 185-acre campus of Michigan State University, compared with a conservatively estimated 370 adults in this area before spraying. In 1954 every robin nest under observation by Mehner produced young. Towards the end of June, 1957, when at least 370 young birds (the normal replacement of the adult population) would have been foraging over the campus in the years before spraying began, Mehner could find only one young robin. A year later Dr. Wallace was to report: 'At no time during the spring or summer (of 1958) did I see a fledgling robin anywhere on the main campus, and so far I have failed to find anyone else who has seen one there.'

Part of this failure to produce young is due, of course, to the fact that one or more of a pair of robins dies before the nesting cycle is completed. But Wallace has significant records which point to something more sinister – the actual destruction of the birds' capacity to reproduce. He has, for example, 'records of robins and other birds building nests but laying no eggs, and others laying eggs and incubating them but not hatching them. We have one record of a robin that sat on its eggs faithfully for twenty-one days and they did not hatch. The normal incubation period is thirteen days …. Our analyses are showing high concentrations of DDT in the testes and ovaries of breeding birds,' [he told a congressional committee in 1960]. 'Ten males had amounts ranging from 30 to 109 parts per

Silent Spring (continued)

million in the testes, and two females had 151 and 211 parts per million respectively in the egg follicles in their ovaries.'

Soon studies in other areas began to develop findings equally dismal. Professor Joseph Hickey and his students at the University of Wisconsin, after careful comparative studies of sprayed and unsprayed areas, reported the robin mortality to be at least 86 to 88 per cent. The Cranbrook Institute of Science at Bloomfield Hills, Michigan, in an effort to assess the extent of bird loss caused by the spraying of the elms, asked in 1956 that all birds thought to be victims of DDT poisoning be turned in to the institute for examination. The request had a response beyond all expectations. Within a few weeks the deep-freeze facilities of the institute were taxed to capacity, so that other specimens had to be refused. By 1959 a thousand poisoned birds from this single community had been turned in or reported. Although the robin was the chief victim (one woman calling the institute reported twelve robins lying dead on her lawn as she spoke), sixty-three different species were included among the specimens examined at the institute.

The robins, then, are only one part of the chain of devastation linked to the spraying of the elms ...

Rachel Carson, *Silent Spring*, Crest Books, 1963

A tale with two endings

Silent Spring was written in 1963. What will be written in 2063?

The following passages act as a link between the *Silent Spring* introduction and the work beyond. They should focus the debate in the present, and lead pupils into an awareness of concerns now.

Tearing up the map of creation

A fish the size of a barn door is on the verge of extinction. But if we failed to notice this until almost too late, how many other species are disappearing? What we do know, says *Tim Radford* is that the massacre of the species at present rates has baleful consequences for Planet Earth.

A big fish is about to swim away forever. The barndoor skate *Raja levis* seems close to extinction. In 1951 research ships found it in 10 per cent of all trawls of the St Pierre Bank in the Atlantic Ocean off Newfoundland. Over the last 20 years, none at all have been caught there. The barndoor skate grows to a metre across, not something you would miss if you were looking out for it. But nobody was. 'Failure to examine historical data has resulted in the largest skate in the North Atlantic being driven to near extinction without anyone noticing,' say researchers. If something the size of a barn door could slip away without being missed 'the fate of little known species is likely to be worse'.

The things that make life possible are barely visible. Laboratory experiments based on small, artificial worlds keep demonstrating that diversity is life's strongest card. The recycling of air and water and plant nutrients is the business of little creatures most of us never notice. The food we eat, the medicines we take and the tools we use have been fashioned for us by 500 million years of evolution. Yet we know practically nothing about most of them. We even lack

Animal detective

A taxonomist classifies organisms. This traditional method of counting species suggests that insects dominate the world's biodiversity. However, new methods – using gene-typing techniques – reveal that single-cell microbes have a greater diversity than insects and plants.

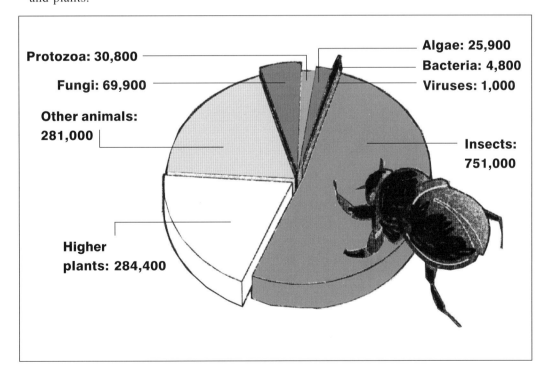

Protozoa: 30,800
Fungi: 69,900
Other animals: 281,000
Higher plants: 284,400
Algae: 25,900
Bacteria: 4,800
Viruses: 1,000
Insects: 751,000

Tearing up the map of creation (continued)

a starting point. Who knows how many small fry are being dished? Creatures are being erased from life's register faster that anyone can record them. All the evidence is that humans are extinguishing other life forms on an epic scale. But there are no tallymen to count the dead or take the measure of the living: there are probably only about 7,000 experts – they are called taxonomists, or sometimes systematists – on the whole planet with the authority to distinguish species one from another. Most are in the wrong places. And few have been getting much encouragement. Without them we cannot even begin arguing.

According to some theorists, half of all the creatures with which humans share the planet could be about to steal away into the eternal night, simply because their homes are being destroyed. By man. The world's dwindling tropical forests could be losing creatures at the rate of 27,000 a year – three creatures an hour – at the most conservative estimate. The precision of these figures is disputed, the truth behind them is not. In the last century, birds and mammals have been disappearing at an average rate of one a year. This is already a thousand times faster than the 'background' rate of extinction. It is confirmed by crude counts made by the conservation groups: a tenth of all flowering plants are about to disappear: a tenth of all birds on the planet are seriously endangered, many of the big mammal groups – the cats, in particular – could be about to disappear. But 99 per cent of creation is less than 3 mm long. Most of smaller species will be gone before scientists ever find out they were here.

Biodiversity is a matter of naked human self-interest. Human economy rests on plants. Crops and their wild relatives have to be understood and conserved and that means the insects that prey on them must also be understood. Plants that provide most medicines – from aspirin for headaches to taxol for breast cancer – have developed the chemicals they possess as a response to their co-evolution with insects. There could be billions of dollars of useful, valuable, exploitable knowledge to be gained from almost unknown creatures in their habitats. Why do barnacles not grow on starfish? Because they secrete a natural anti-fouling paint. Why do arctic fish not freeze? Because they have an antifreeze fluid to keep blood circulating. Last year Cornell scientists calculated that if humans had to pay for the services they received free from nature – pollination, water purification, crop pest control, that sort of thing – the bill would be $2.9 million million annually. Fellow creatures are a kind of map of creation. 'Just knowing how many species there are is like having proper maps of the stars', says John Lawton. 'It's exactly the same for a proper science of ecology and evolution and many areas of biology. We need to know how many organisms there are, what they are and where they are.'

The Guardian, 11 August 1998; © The Guardian

Tearing up the map of creation (continued)

Natural remedies

Like many drugs, aspirin was developed after scientists began to analyse chemical constituents of plants used in traditional, herbal healing. Called the ethnobotanical approach, it may uncover future drug treatments.

Drug	Medical use	Plant source
Aspirin	Reduce pain and inflammation	*Filipendula ulmaria*
Codeine	Ease pain; suppress coughing	*Papaver somniferum*
Ipecac	Induce vomiting	*Psychotria ipecacuanha*
Pilocarpine	Reduce eye pressure	*Pilocarpus jaborandi*
Pseudocephedrine	Reduce nasal congestion	*Ephedra sinica*
Quinine	Combat malaria	*Cinchona pubescens*
Reserpine	Lower blood pressure	*Rauwolfia serpentina*
Scopolamine	Ease motion sickness	*Datura stramonium*
Theophylline	Open bronchial passages	*Camellia sinesis*
Vinblastine	Combat Hodgkin's disease	*Catharathus roseus*

Clean-up to bring new life to dirtiest river

By Mike Merritt

It is Scotland's dirtiest river. Many miles of its length are so badly polluted that it is bereft of all life.

But the Almond, the West Lothian river which, ironically, flows through three scenic country parks, is to be the subject of a multi-million pound clean-up and the move is likely to become the model for action over other polluted rivers in Scotland.

A conference of environmental groups, government agencies, local councils and voluntary organisations in Linlithgow this week will begin the fightback by endorsing a 120-page plan which is the culmination of four years' work.

Within 15 years, it is hoped to have salmon and trout running the river's 31 miles from its source in the Cant Hills in North Lanarkshire through West Lothian and into the Firth of Forth at Cramond, near Edinburgh. Wildlife will flourish again and anglers and canoeists will be able to use the river.

The Almond has ranked as one of Scotland's most historic rivers since the Romans set up a supply base for the construction of the Antonine Wall on its banks at Cramond in the second century.

Conservationists claim the Almond is unique in Scotland in that it has suffered the effects of two industrial revolutions – one last century and one in the last 50 years.

The development of the coal and oil-shale mining industries last century has had the greatest consequences on the river. Waste water run-off from the shale bings and mines poured sulphuric acid and iron into the river, turning certain stretches orange and suffocating life. In the second half of this century, the growth of towns, such as Livingston, and the electronics industry had the greatest impact. Sewage and rain water made toxic by rubber, oil and metals from roads and car parks have also killed large parts of the Almond.

Despite its high pollution levels, experts say the Almond is not beyond salvation. The new plan will build on improvements already under way, such as a £100m sewage scheme being built by East of Scotland Water. Anti-pollution measures are also being installed by various other bodies, including the Coal Authority. Some companies are even sponsoring the construction of 'wetland' areas to collect surface water run-off and naturally filter it before it reaches the Almond. No government money has been put directly into the project – although agencies such as Scottish Natural Heritage are committing their own funds.

The proposed EU water framework directive will require river catchment planning for all of Scotland's rivers – and that will almost certainly mean government cash will be needed.

Peter Pollard, the river valley's officer for the Scottish Wildlife Trust, which is coordinating the project, believes the Almond can be a clean river again. 'The river has a reputation as Scotland's dirtiest,' he said. 'The scenic areas of the river corridor stand in stark contrast to lengthy sections of water that is biologically dead. Over the next few years we will be looking for indicators that we are winning the battle.'

Scotland on Sunday, 31 May 1998

READING

Close reading

Teachers' introduction

Instead of pupils simply launching into past papers or a series of disconnected reading passages, the reading work below is devised to cover at least three areas of biodiversity.

Reading is not simply the decoding of phonics or visual recall of words. A good definition of reading is 'understanding what has been written down'. This definition helps pupils to move away from the panic of thinking themselves incapable of doing the work simply because they do not understand every word. They learn to grasp the gist from the context and, thus, they are able to find their way into understanding what has been written.

Explaining this use of the word 'reading' is time well spent.

The passages below have questions that determine understanding of:
• vocabulary
• the argument of the passage
• the style of the writing
• the structure.

Explaining to pupils the purpose of the questions makes the task less opaque. They can then define a question as a 'vocabulary question' or a 'structure question', and this focuses them on to what precisely they should do to answer correctly. This precision, of course, is crucial in the Standard Grade exam and at Higher.

These passages are not designed as a series of silent writing tests, but as formative devices in teaching close reading and understanding the writer's craft. The early passages are best tackled in groups, or teacher led, and the answers to the later passages could be written.

Within each level, the passages vary in difficulty. This is deliberate in order to reach as many pupils as possible. The teacher must select the passages that best suit the pupils. Some passages may appear very easy: they could be used as a stepping stone to the more difficult in each level. Some may appear too difficult. They are designed to stretch the most able pupils to the level beyond – including, of course, Higher. The long passages are specifically geared to Higher pupils, who must learn to cope with long and complicated arguments, necessary to more advanced study. In short, the thinking underpinning the reading passages is not that of the summative assessment: rather it belongs to more contemplative education.

At the end of each level, there is one summative assessment laid out on Higher Still lines. Of course, the 'Reading', 'Writing' and 'Talk' tasks need not be kept separate. Cross-referencing is valid and desirable between the sections. The assessments are printed in sections for convenience, not for prescriptive teaching.

A practical note: to save on photocopying costs, pupils should write the answers in their exercise books rather than on the printed sheets. One class set is thereby reusable.

The following passage could be used for all three levels orally as a way of linking the topic of biodiversity and the process of close reading.

The teacher should go through the questions with pupils showing them how to tackle passages with difficult vocabulary, and unfamiliar ideas.

Mussel ban is just for starters

P1   From today, the 2000-year-old tradition of fishing for freshwater pearls has been banned. Even the handful of so-called 'professional' pearl fisherman in Scotland, who claim to be able to open a mussel with tongs, check it for pearls, and return it to the water without causing any damage, will face penalties of £5000 per mussel if found guilty of intentionally disturbing or selling freshwater pearl mussels.

P2   They argue that the legislation, announced yesterday by Environment Minister Michael Meacher, should have made special provision for licensing responsible pearl fisherman, penalising instead the 'day-trippers' and 'amateurs' who, they claim, have wreaked such damage on Britain's fragile population of fresh water mussels.

P3   The Government's conservation agencies, however, backed by one of the country's leading freshwater mussel experts, Dr Mark Young, of Aberdeen University's zoology department, argue that decline in mussel populations has been so great in recent years that a blanket ban must be imposed.

P4   The ban is one of a series of extensions to the Wildlife and Countryside Act 1981 which gives protection to endangered animals and plants. Until now, it was an offence under the Act to kill or harm mussels, although the examination of mussels was in itself still legal. While charges under the Act are currently pending against a woman at Inverness Sheriff Court, there have been very few prosecutions, despite the police Operation Necklace last year. Experts suggest this is partly because the mussels are found in remote parts of the country, and also because the 'halfway house' type of protection that has been in place till now has been hard to police, and often confusing for law-enforcers.

P5   Wildlife groups and conservationists have greeted Mr Meacher's list of new species and extensions of protections with delight. The Scottish Wildlife Trust said it was delighted that a ban had now been put on the trade in wild bulbs of the wild hyacinth, or bluebell. Ironically, conservation-minded gardeners have often sought to plant bluebells, not realising that the bulbs they buy may be depleting wild stocks. They will now be encouraged to buy commercially propagated bulbs which are readily available.

P6   Basking sharks and water voles are among the species which have now been added to Schedule 5 of the Act. A SWT spokesman said it hoped that the new protection afforded the basking shark would lead to its being given greater protection under the United Nations' CITES agreement.

P7   The new protection will come into force for more than 30 native UK species in 21 days' time but the freshwater pearl mussel will gain immediate protection because of fears that unscrupulous fishers would plunder as many stocks as they could if given three weeks' notice.

P8   Scottish Natural Heritage, the Government's conservation agency in Scotland, is stressing that its backing for full protection for the freshwater mussel should not be seen as criticism in any way of skilled traditional pearl fishers and is, in fact, aimed at saving the traditional activity.

P9   A spokesman said: 'The mussels are now in such a precarious state, we cannot afford to take chances with any sort of fishing for the time being. Once stocks have recovered, we may be able to consider a return to sustainable pearl fishing.'

P10   Nevertheless, historical records show that pearl fishing has gone on in Britain for 2000 years. Pliny wrote of Britain's freshwater pearls, and, according to some accounts, it was the renown of these fisheries in Corn-

Mussel ban is just for starters (continued)

wall that persuaded Julius Caesar to lead his army into Britain.

P11 The Stuart Kings had Conservators of Pearls on rivers, and the Scottish freshwater pearls were much beloved by the Victorians. The jewellers Cairncross of Perth is one of the foremost retailers of Scottish freshwater pearl jewellery. Its general manager, Martin Young, believes a system would have been sufficient to save the stocks from 'fly-by-night fishermen' while still allowing bona fide fishers and shops to continue.

P12 He said: 'These indigenous pearls come in beautiful colours and shapes and sizes. We bring them to their glory when we put them into items of jewellery and they are affordable – £135 upwards.'

P13 He admitted that such items could now go up in price, but as nobody would be offering them for sale, nobody would be buying them. Both he and professional pearl fisherman Steven McCormick believe that by licensing 'professional' fishermen, the Government could

also have ensured that the health of rivers was monitored and mussel stocks reported on.

P14 Mr McCormick, a fourth-generation pearl fisher, blames not only those who have no interest in the long-term future of the freshwater mussel for its destruction, but also many landowners for failing to manage rivers properly and allowing nitrate run-off and other forms of pollution to damage this highly sensitive stock. He believes that the decline of the mussel is part of the same cycle of the decline in salmon and trout stocks as the populations depend for their healthy breeding on each other.

P15 Dr Young, however, who is carrying out a national survey of freshwater mussels for SNH and has been studying the species since 1978, is convinced that over-exploitation is the main cause of the decimation of stocks in recent years.

P16 His initial advice to the Government when he first began his survey work was that partial protection would be adequate. But his recent

survey work has revealed 'a substantial further decline' in the mussel population 'to the point where there are literally only a handful of rivers left in Scotland, and only one in Wales and one in England, where there are what you would call healthy reproducing populations of mussels'.

P17 'To my great disappointment, on a number of rivers, including the Spey, mussel kills had occurred where mussels had been opened with tongs – so even the use of tongs has not been saving the mussel. Therefore, I formed the view that full protection was needed,' he said.

P18 He hopes that in time, stocks will have recovered to the extent that a limited number of fishermen can be licensed. But mussels can take from 20 years upwards to reproduce and such a prospect is likely to be 'tens of years rather than five years' from now.

P19 The question, when and if that time comes, is whether traditional pearl-fishing skills will still exist.

The Herald, 27 March 1998

Pupils' support notes

You may not understand all of the words in the passage, but will probably understand the drift of it.

Here are questions and strategies that will help you to find a way into this passage.

Step 1
Read the passage over quickly.

Step 2
Read it again in sections.

To find the 'sections' think about where each new argument or line of thinking begins. Mark it on the sheet, or note it on paper.

Step 3
Think.

What is the passage actually saying?

Step 4
Look at all your sections. How do they fit together to deliver what the passage is saying? (What, for example, has the bluebells point to do with the pearl fishers?)

Step 5
Paragraph 12 begins 'He said:'. 'He' refers to Martin Young in the previous paragraph. Can you find another example of a word that connects two paragraphs?

Step 6
A writer chooses words very carefully to make clear his or her point of view. In paragraph 1, the writer has chosen to say 'so-called "professional" pearl fishermen': she shows she does not agree with them by the use of the word 'so-called' and by the use of the inverted commas round 'professional'.

Can you find another example of writing where the words show the writer's point of view?

Step 7
Although you might not know every word in a passage, it is possible to understand the passage by looking for clues around the unfamiliar word.

In paragraph 16 the text says that Dr Young thought 'partial protection' would be adequate. But his recent survey work has revealed 'a substantial further decline' in the mussel population 'to the point where there are literally only a handful of rivers left in Scotland, and only one in Wales, and one in England, where there are what you would call healthy reproducing populations of mussels'.

What does 'partial' mean?

Look at the word for a possible clue.

Look around the word and think what this paragraph is saying. Dr Young is saying that there has been protection but, nevertheless, the situation is getting worse. There are fewer mussel beds than in the past.

What then does 'partial' mean?

It means 'some', 'a part', 'a section'.

There has only been some protection, which has caused the decrease in mussels.

Can you find a word you don't know and work out its meaning?

These steps help you to understand how to find:
- the purpose of a passage
- the underlying structure
- the connecting words
- the meaning of difficult words
- the specialised use of language.

Now you are ready to tackle passages in groups or on your own.

Foundation reading passages

The first four reading passages are all about birds and the questions require pupils to:
- read with understanding
- answer questions on vocabulary
- follow the structure of the passage
- comment on the argument of the four passages as a unit
- comment on the writer's craft.

The remaining passages deal with other environmental issues and require pupils to understand:
- different writing styles
- juxtaposition of words and images
- how an idea can be sustained over a range of writing styles.

The summative passage and summative assessment are difficult for many Foundation pupils, and are probably suitable only for the most able. Passage F8 and its related questions could be used as a summative assessment for less able Foundation pupils.

Passage F1

BIRDS KILLED OFF BY GARDEN TITBITS

by Jonathan Leake, Environment Correspondent

P1 BRITAIN'S favourite garden birds are being devastated by an epidemic of food poisoning caused by the titbits left out by householders. Tens of thousands of house sparrows and greenfinches have been killed by salmonella, with some people finding up to 30 dead birds scattered around their gardens.

P2 Trichomoniasis, a parasitic disease, is destroying a population of collar doves and wood pigeons, and a third micro-organism, so far unidentified, has killed tens of thousands of blue tits in the past few weeks.

P3 James Kirkwood, chief vet at London Zoo, who is coordinating an investigation into the cause of the deaths, said they appeared to be happening across Britain with certain species in danger of being wiped out in some areas.

P4 He believed one of the main causes was the growing number of people feeding birds in their back gardens, which meant diseases could easily jump between species and individual birds. 'When they gather together at bird tables they can contaminate food that is then eaten by other individuals. It is very sad because they take a long time to die and it is quite painful', said Kirkwood.

P5 Professor Chris Perrins, director of the Edward Grey Institute of Field Ornithology at Oxford University, said some bird-lovers could also be accidentally poisoning birds by giving them mouldy food – particularly nuts.

Based on an article in *The Sunday Times*, 9 June 1996

Questions on passage F1 – Birds killed off by garden titbits

1. What is the purpose of this piece of writing? Is it to entertain the reader, or to give information?

2. Look carefully at paragraphs 2 and 3.

    (a) How widespread are the deaths of the birds?

    (b) Do you think the writer thinks this is serious?

    (c) Give a reason for your answer.

3. Paragraph 5 contains an unexpected idea. It does not seem to fit the rest of the article. Can you explain what is unexpected about it?

4. Look back to paragraph 1.

    (a) What does the word 'salmonella' mean?

    (b) What appears in paragraph 1 that helps you to know this?

5. Do you think that readers are meant to feel sorry for the birds? Write down words that suggest this.

Passage F2

Falcons under threat

By James McGhee, Environment Reporter

Rare Lothian Birds could be wiped out by an invasion of European egg-thieves.

The alert was issued today after a tip-off to the RSPB that thieves are taking orders from abroad for Scottish peregrine falcon eggs and chicks.

The threat could push the bird of prey back to the brink of extinction in Lothian.

Edinburgh's chief RSPB investigator Dave Dick said: 'We're worried. We hear there are orders out for Scottish peregrines from abroad where the Scottish peregrine is in great demand.'

The rare birds sell on the black market at £400–£600 each; making a clutch worth around £2000.

Myth

'There is a myth that the Scottish birds are the best hunters,' said Mr Dick.

The alert was sounded two days ago when known egg thieves were spotted checking out a Highland area with a history of golden eagle egg thefts.

Spotted sitting in a car by members of a local bird group, the two men from England were interviewed by police and found to have records.

'It is a bit early but often these people will be out before egg-laying so they can make their plans,' said Mr Dick.

George Carse, a peregrine specialist with Lothian Raptor Group, said that although there were seven pairs of the birds in Lothian, thefts and killings meant they were not increasing as they should.

'They have come back from the brink of extinction here in the last 15 years but they are very much at risk from thieves,' he said.

'So far they are holding their own.

Problem

'But they are not increasing much and if the problem goes on at the present rate, the number will be cut by at least half.'

Sgt Malcolm Henderson, one of two wildlife liaison officers with Lothian and Borders Police, said: 'There is quite a bit of money involved in egg-stealing.'

Sgt Henderson was speaking today at the Scottish Police Wildlife Liaison Officers annual conference in Glasgow.

Foreign threat: a Scottish peregrine falcon

Evening News, 1996

Questions on passage F2 – Falcons under threat

1. Look at the headline to the passage.

    (a) Are readers meant to feel sympathy for the falcons?
       (tick one)
       YES

       NO

    (b) How do you know this?

2. From the introductory section, write down two words that also tell you how readers are meant to feel about the falcons.

3. Look at the section entitled 'Myth'. Explain what is happening to the falcons.

4. Look at the section entitled 'Problem'. Why might the writer have included the comment from Sgt Malcolm Henderson?

5. Look back at the introductory section and at the words underneath the picture. Apart from the danger to the falcons, the writer is suggesting another idea about the egg thieves. What is it?

Passage F3

NEST WATCH DRAMA AS OSPREY EGGS SNATCHED FROM HIGH-RISE HAVEN

S1 It was an operation carried out with military precision. In broad daylight the thieves scaled the 40ft high Scots pine wearing spiked climbing boots to get at the target – an osprey's nest.

Three eggs, due to hatch in less than a fortnight's time, were snatched. Now security surrounding more than 100 osprey nests has been stepped up following the daring raid in the Highlands.

S2 The theft was discovered at noon on Sunday by Allan Bantick, a local volunteer, who regularly watches the site to guard against intruders.

Mr Bantick, 57, said: 'I was surprised to see that the birds were not on the nest. Then they flew over and looked in. They shuffled about and fidgeted for a while, then flew away again. That is not the behaviour of birds with eggs to look after.'

When he realised what had happened, Mr Bantick called the police, who checked the nest. Yesterday a spokesman for Northern Constabulary said: 'This person must be caught. Often these crimes are committed by a group together, who do not stop at just one nest. They may be stealing to order for a wealthy egg collector and could well strike again.'

S3 The nest has been used since 1982 and last year the same birds successfully raised one healthy chick.

Richard Thaxton, warden at the most famous osprey site at Boat of Garten, Inverness-shire, said yesterday: 'It is a despicable thing to do. The embryos in these eggs were well developed and would have hatched in a very short time.'

Abridged from *The Daily Mail*, 13 May 1997

Questions on passage F3 – Nest watch drama as osprey eggs snatched from high-rise haven

1. Using your own words explain how the egg theft was discovered.

    Mr Bantick   _____

    He noticed   _____

    He then   _____

2. In Section 3 the warden, Richard Thaxton, explains why he thinks the egg theft is despicable.

    (a) What is his reason?

    (b) What do you think 'despicable' means?

3. Look back at Section 1.

    (a) Do you think the thieves were well organised?

    (b) What phrase tells you this?

    (c) The first paragraph introduces the story. It has been written in a very unusual and interesting way. Look carefully at it and suggest why the writer might have written it in this way.

Passage F4

Invernest Caley!
Bird lays egg in club's car park

P1 A stray bird is causing headaches before a football celebration bash – after setting up home in a club's car park.

P2 The wayward oystercatcher scraped a nest in the gravel and laid two eggs at Inverness Caledonian Thistle's new stadium in the town's Longman area.

P3 And that is set to cause chaos before tonight's glamour friendly against Premier League Aberdeen to mark Thistle's title triumph.

P4 Concerned club chiefs have coned off the blundering bird's nest.

P5 But up to 3,000 fans could be turned away from the car park as bird watchdogs keep an eagle eye on the situation.

P6 A spokesman for the Royal Society for the Protection of Birds rapped: 'It is illegal to destroy the nest and moving the eggs is not an option.'

P7 Caley Thistle commercial manager and star player Charlie Christie groaned: 'It could really cause a problem for the game.'

Questions on passage F4 – Invernest Caley! Bird lays egg in club's car park

1. This passage is different from the other three. In what ways is it different?

    (1)

    (1)

2. Why are 'bird watchdogs keeping an eye on the situation'? Give two reasons.

    (1)

    (1)

3. Paragraph 3 begins with 'And'.

    (a) Suggest a reason why the writer has done this.

    (1)

    (b) Give your opinion of this style of writing.

    (1)

4. The writer has used the same type of connecting word elsewhere in the passage.

    (a) Identify the word and its use.

    (1)

    (b) Comment on its use.

    (1)

5. Comment on the use of 'bash' in paragraph 1.

    (1)

Questions on passages F1–F4

1. All four passages have been built up in the same way.

    - The headline is first.
    - The main event is in paragraph 1.
    - The detail is developed in the middle of each article.
    - There is a quotation at the end.

    Fill in the grid on the next page from the information in all the passages. This is the shape of a news story that you can look at again in the writing unit.

2. A news story usually has a photo. Two of the articles have had their photos removed. Look at those with photos and those without and suggest why news stories normally have photos.

    Leaving aside the content of the articles, think about how they were written. Were they funny? Were they sad? Were they serious? Put them into order of how well you liked the writing and explain the reasons for your 'league table'.

    (1) Top of my league table was …

         because …

    (2)

    (3)

    (4)

Passage	Headlines	Main Point	Detail	Quotations
F1				
F2				
F3				
F4				

Passage F5

The previous four passages were newspaper articles about birds. The next passage is about the effect of human consumption on the planet. Consumption means 'taking'. Humans take more and more, and in the process are destroying the planet. The passage is from a book entitled *Rescue Mission Planet Earth*.

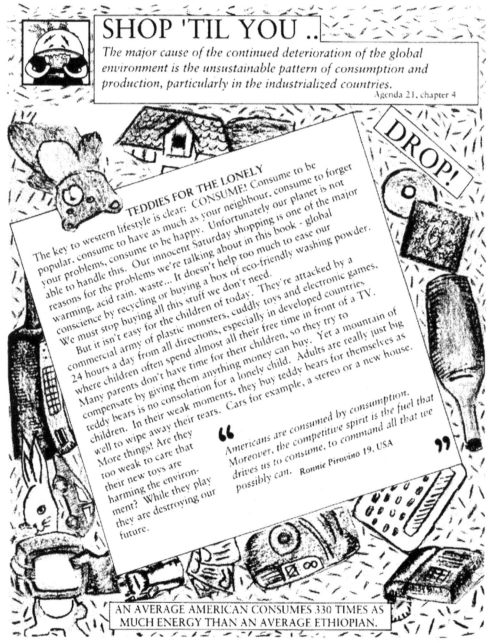

SHOP 'TIL YOU ..

The major cause of the continued deterioration of the global environment is the unsustainable pattern of consumption and production, particularly in the industrialized countries.

Agenda 21, chapter 4

DROP!

TEDDIES FOR THE LONELY

The key to western lifestyle is clear: CONSUME! Consume to be popular, consume to have as much as your neighbour, consume to forget your problems, consume to be happy. Unfortunately our planet is not able to handle this. Our innocent Saturday shopping is one of the major reasons for the problems we're talking about in this book - global warming, acid rain, waste... It doesn't help too much to ease our conscience by recycling or buying a box of eco-friendly washing powder. We must stop buying all this stuff we don't need.

But it isn't easy for the children of today. They're attacked by a commercial army of plastic monsters, cuddly toys and electronic games, 24 hours a day from all directions, especially in developed countries where children often spend almost all their free time in front of a TV. Many parents don't have time for their children, so they try to compensate by giving them anything money can buy. Yet a mountain of teddy bears is no consolation for a lonely child. Adults are really just big children. In their weak moments, they buy teddy bears for themselves as well to wipe away their tears. Cars for example, a stereo or a new house. More things! Are they too weak to care that their new toys are harming the environment? While they play they are destroying our future.

" *Americans are consumed by consumption. Moreover, the competitive spirit is the fuel that drives us to consume, to command all that we possibly can.* Ronnie Pirovino 19, USA "

AN AVERAGE AMERICAN CONSUMES 330 TIMES AS MUCH ENERGY THAN AN AVERAGE ETHIOPIAN.

Rescue Mission Planet Earth

Questions on passage F5 – Teddies for the lonely

1. There are two points in the first paragraph of 'Teddies for the Lonely'. What are they?

    (1)

    (1)

2. In the second paragraph the writer explains why it is difficult for children to take the solution he suggests at the end of the first paragraph. What reason does he give for this?

    (1)

3. The writer goes on to make two points about adults. What are they?

    (1)

    (1)

4. Explain the link the writer is making between teddies and cars.

    (1)

5. Look at the words at the bottom of the page. How do they tie in with the ideas in 'Teddies for the Lonely'?

    (1)

6. Now look at the 'Shop 'til you …' box at the top of the page. What point is the writer making about shopping?

    (1)

7. Now consider the design of the page.

    (a) What has been drawn around the words?

    (1)

    (b) Can you suggest a reason why?

    (1)

8. Why is the word 'drop' falling over?

    (1)

Passage F6

Read the passage 'Turning up the Heat', and then answer the following questions.

TURNING UP THE HEAT

We are addicted to energy. We want to buy more, newer, bigger, better things; we want to drive all over in our own cars; we want to fly whenever it's possible. This comfortable life costs energy and the more we use, the bigger the threat to the environment. The use of fossil fuel (coal, oil, gas) results in acid rain and the greenhouse effect: hurricanes, floods and the rising of the sea level. These threats are serious. The sea level is rising at ten times its natural speed. This can result in whole countries disappearing! Still fossil fuels are the most popular energy source. It's hard to use less. Nuclear power has failed to provide a safe alternative. The big question is what happens when developing countries start requiring the luxuries enjoyed in the developed world? If we used as much energy per person as industrialized countries, the world would need five times as much as it uses today. Our planet definitely couldn't stand the pollution this would generate. So what should we in the developing world do? Shut up, stay poor. No way! We must find new *sustainable* sources of energy and so must the industrialized countries.

Rescue Mission Planet Earth
© Peace Child International 1994. Reproduced by permission of
Kingfisher Publications PLC. All rights reserved.

Questions on passage F6 – Turning up the heat

1. Look first of all at the design of the page. Why is it so bold?

    (1)

2. (a) In the book from which this passage was taken, colour was used. What colours do you imagine were used?

    (1)

    (b) Can you suggest a reason for your choice of colour?

    (1)

3. Read the passage through. Divide it into the four points the writer is making about energy.

    (a) We use …

    (1)

    (b) Nuclear power …

    (1)

    (c) When the developing countries …

    (2)

    (d) The solution is …

    (1)

Passage F7

Biodiversity is a word made from the words 'biological' and 'diversity'. Biological is to do with living things and diversity means differentness. Biodiversity means the variety of life. Look at the page printed below, and read the whole page.

At the top are three lines of very *formal* writing. Then there is less formal *non-fiction* writing, and at the bottom a piece of *creative* writing.

PROBLEM FAMILY

Biological resources feed and clothe us, provide us with housing, medicines and spiritual nourishment. The loss of biodiversity continues at a faster rate as a result of human activity.

Agenda 21, chapter 15

What is Biodiversity? Bio means life, as in Biology, the science of life. Diversity means variety so biodiversity means the variety of life - 30 million species according to one estimate. Trouble is, one species seems intent on wiping out the other 29,999,999. People need what plants and animals provide: for example, a drug that comes from the rose-colored periwinkle of Madagascar, has helped many people recover from leukaemia (a kind of cancer). By our lack of respect for other life forms around us, we are gradually killing the ecosystems that give us life.

3.

Senya Perebaeva, 12, Russia

Mother Nature
I am mother nature,
the lasting habitat of destruction
I am a creation of heaven, from heaven I am
given for man to dwell and to toil.
But man, in complete disregard of truth, has
chosen to destroy all my children.
Greed and hate, the nagging times of age,
have flamed the heart of man.
The ravages of war and factory are
the friendly foe of man.
The young earth's fervant destroyer is
the fumes of the factory.
The water animals happily sing the songs of life,
while we send our nets to fish their families
in entirety.
But know you not man that in your greed you
may destroy all my off springs?
Yet in destroying me, you pave a smooth way to
your own destruction.
Repent now from your greed and protect the
sons and daughters of mother nature.
The value of a shade will not be known until
the tree is cut down.
Sheku Kamara, 20, Sierra Leone

Rescue Mission Planet Earth

Questions on passage F7 – Problem family

1.   The three passages on this page are making the same point. What is it?

(1)

2.   The point is being made by different means. How is each being made?

(a) In the first part it is made by

(1)

(b) In the second part it is made by

(1)

(c) In 'Mother Nature' it is made by

(1)

3.   On the previous pages you have studied passages about birds, shopping and energy. Can you think how these separate topics are linked up with each other and with the three sections on passage F7?

(a) They are linked up with each other by …

(2)

(b) They are linked up with this page by …

(2)

4.   Through studying all these passages, what ideas have been new to you? Have you thought about the Earth? What can we humans do to alter the situation?

Passage F8

THE GOOD STEWARD

I dream of a world in which people want to save the rose-colored periwinkle of Madagascar for its own sake, not because it happens to contain a cure for cancer in people.

Children's State of the Planet Handbook 1992

BIODIVERSITY CONVENTION

A lot of these ideas are included in the Biodiversity Convention which will soon become a law. 142 countries signed the Convention at Rio but it doesn't become a law until at least 30 countries *ratify* it - that is make it a law in their own countries. By August 1993, 26 countries had ratified it. The USA signed it in April 1993.

AGENDA 21 SAYS:
- one thing: SAVE IT!! In order to do that, *governments have to:*
• Create a world information resource for biodiversity.
• Protect biodiversity! This should be a part of all government plans on environment and development.
• Offer indigenous peoples the chance to contribute to biodiversity conservation.
• Make sure that poor countries share equally in the commercial exploitation of their products and experience.
• Protect and repair damaged habitats; conserve endangered species.
• Assess every big project - dams, roads etc. - for its environmental impact.

Rescue Mission Planet Earth

Questions on passage F8 – The good steward

1. This passage also has three sections to it but they have a different purpose. What is the purpose of each piece of writing, and why are they combined on one page?

    (2)

2. How does the picture at the bottom emphasise this?

    (1)

Reflection
Looking at the passages overall, it is easy to think that biodiversity only affects people living in the countryside. From your reading of all the passages, what has biodiversity to do with city dwellers?

Summative reading passage (Foundation)

The following piece of writing appeared in the *Daily Mail* on 1 June 1999. It explains how Prince Charles was concerned about genetically modified organisms (GMOs) and set about finding out public opinion on this through the internet.

'GMO' is the scientific name for the material in genetically modified food, which is food that has been created by science, not naturally grown.

Read the passage below and answer the questions in your own words.

GENETICALLY MODIFIED ORGANISMS
An article by the Prince of Wales

Summary

P1   The debate about the use of GM technology continues, with daily news of claims about the safety or the risks. The public's reaction shows instinctive nervousness about tampering with nature when we don't know all the consequences. There are unanswered questions that need to be asked – about the need for GM food, its safety, the environmental consequences, consumer choice and the usefulness to feed the world's growing population.

P2   At the end of last year I set up a discussion forum on my website on the question of GMOs. I wanted to encourage wider public debate about what I see as a fundamental issue and one that affects each and every one of us and future generations.

P3   There was a huge response – some 10,000 replies have indicated that public concern about the use of GM technology has been growing. Many food producers and retailers have clearly felt the same overwhelming anxiety from their consumers who are demanding a choice in what they eat. A number of them have now banned GM ingredients from their own-brand products.

P4   But the debate continues to rage. Not a day goes by without some new piece of research claiming to demonstrate either the safety or the risks of GM technology. It is very hard for people to know just who is right. Few of us are able to interpret all the scientific information that is available – and even the experts don't always agree. But what I believe the public's reaction shows is that instinctively we are nervous about tampering with nature when we can't be sure that we know enough about all the consequences.

P5   Having followed this debate very closely for some while now, I believe that there are still a number of unanswered questions that need to be asked.

P6   ***1.   Do we need GM food in this country?***
On the basis of what we have seen so far, we don't appear to need it at all. The benefits, such as there are, seem to be limited to the people who own the technology and the people who farm on an industrialised scale. We are constantly told that this technology may have huge benefits for the future.

Summative reading passage (continued)

Well, perhaps, but we have all heard claims like that before and they don't always come true in the long run – look at the case of antibiotic growth promoters in animal feedstuff ...

P7   *2. Is GM food safe for us to eat?*

There is certainly no evidence to the contrary. But how much evidence do we have? And are we looking at the right things? The major decisions about what can be grown and what can be sold are taken on the basis of studying what is known about the original plant, comparing it to the genetically modified variety, and then deciding whether the two are 'substantially equivalent'. But is it enough to look only at what is already known? Isn't there at least a possibility that the new crops (particularly those that have been made resistant to antibiotics) will behave in unexpected ways, producing toxic or allergic reactions? Only independent scientific research, over a long period, can provide the final answer.

P8   *3. Why are the rules for approving GM foods so much less stringent than those for new medicines produced using the same technology?*

Before drugs are released into the marketplace they have to undergo the most rigorous testing – and quite right too. But GM food is also designed in a laboratory for human consumption, albeit in different circumstances. Surely it is equally important that we are confident that it will do us no harm?

P9   *4. Is it sensible to plant test crops without strict regulations in place?*

Such crops are being planted in this country now – under a voluntary code of practice. But English Nature, the Government's official adviser on nature conservation, has argued that we ought to put strict, enforceable regulations in place first. Even then, will it really be possible to prevent contamination of nearby wildlife or crops, whether organic or not? Since bees and the wind don't obey any sort of rules – voluntary or statutory – we shall soon have an unprecedented and unethical situation in which one farmer's crops will contaminate another's against his will.

P10 *5. How will consumers be able to exercise genuine choice?*

Labelling schemes clearly have a role to play. But if conventional and organic crops can become contaminated by GM crops grown nearby, those people who wish to be sure they are eating or growing absolutely natural, non-industrialised, *real* food, will be denied that choice. This seems to me to be wrong.

P11 *6. Are GM crops really the only way to feed the world's growing population?*

This argument sounds suspiciously like emotional blackmail to me. Is there any serious academic research to substantiate such a sweeping statement? The countries that might be expected to benefit certainly take a different

Summative reading passage (continued)

view. Representatives of 20 African states, including Ethiopia, have published a statement denying that gene technologies will 'help farmers to produce the food that is needed in the 21st century'. On the contrary, they 'think it will destroy the diversity, the local knowledge and the sustainable agricultural systems … and undermine our capacity to feed ourselves'. How much more could we achieve if all the research funds currently devoted to fashionable GM techniques – which run into billions of dollars a year – were applied to improving methods of agriculture that have stood the test of time? We already know that yields from many traditional farming systems can be doubled, at least, by making better use of existing natural resources.

Daily Mail, 1 May 1999

Summative reading assessment (Foundation)

Section A – Understanding

1.   Look at paragraph 3. What two pieces of evidence suggest that people are very worried about the issue of genetically modified food?

(2)

2.   Look at paragraph 6.

(a) Who benefits from GM foods?

(2)

(b) What has been suggested about antibiotic growth producers?

(2)

3.   Look at paragraph 8. How does Prince Charles link the situation with medical drugs to the situation with GM foods?

(2)

4.   Look at paragraph 9. Explain in your own words how the wind and bees make regulations impossible to enforce.

(2)

5.   (a) In paragraph 11 the hungry people of the Third World are discussed. What is the attitude of the Third World to GM food?

(2)

(b) What arguments do the representatives of the 20 African states put forward to support their views?

(2)

14

Section B – Analysis

6.   From paragraph 2 write down two words that emphasise strength of feelings.

(2)

7.   In paragraph 6, the sentence 'Well, perhaps' appears. Why does Prince Charles put this in and what does it add to the point he is making?

(2)

8.   In paragraph 7 there are a number of questions. Why has Prince Charles written it this way, rather than tell the readers what he wants them to know?

(2)

9.   In paragraph 10, Prince Charles talks of '*real* food'.

      (a) What does he mean by this and which words help you to understand this?

(2)

      (b) Why is 'real' in italics?

(2)

$$\overline{10}$$

Section C – Evaluation

10.   (a) For whom is this article written?

- The general public?
- The experts?
- Farmers?

(b) Explain clearly how this is obvious from:
- what is said
- how it is written.

(2)

11.   The passage is set up as 'question and answer'. Does this make it easier to follow or more difficult? Give a reason for your answer.

(1)

12.   (a) What is the attitude of Prince Charles to GM food?

(1)

(b) Explain clearly how you know.

(2)

13.   Has the passage affected your view on the subject? Give a reason for your answer.

(2)

8

Total 32

General reading passages

The first three passages are about birds and the questions require pupils to:
- read with understanding
- answer questions on vocabulary
- follow the structure of the passage
- comment on the argument of the three passages as a unit
- comment on the writer's craft.

The remaining passages deal with other environmental issues, and require pupils to understand:
- different writing styles
- juxtaposition of words and images
- how an idea can be sustained over a range of writing styles.

Passage G1

FEARS AS NUMBERS OF HEN HARRIERS PLUMMET

by Geraldine Murray and David Love

P1 The hen harrier is now believed to be rarer than the corncrake, the official number one protection priority of the Royal Society for the Protection of Birds. A survey has been ordered to determine the exact numbers.

P2 A review a decade ago found 670 breeding pairs in Scotland, but there are fears that this figure may have fallen well below 500. England has only 30 breeding pairs.

P3 RSPB spokesman, Colin Crook, said: 'Illegal persecution by landowners is still one of the main reasons for the decline of the hen harrier. It is crucial that we stop gamekeepers killing the harrier on their grouse moorland. If we achieve this, we can double numbers in five years.

P4 'But, at the same time, we will be protecting the economy of the Highlands. Wildlife tourism is a growth industry and more and more people are coming to Scotland to see its rich variety of wildlife.'

P5 Worries about the harrier are increasing as the RSPB publishes a report this week, which will show that more than 100 reports of crimes against birds of prey in Scotland last year resulted in only one conviction.

P6 The RSPB dealt with 209 reports of offences against wild birds, with more than half involving birds of prey. But despite evidence of abuse of poison and deliberate persecution, only three prosecutions followed. In one, a gamekeeper was convicted of setting a spring trap in the open. The other two cases are still awaiting an outcome.

P7 More than 20 reports of poisoning were confirmed and the RSPB is concerned that four of these cases involved the red kite, of which there are fewer than 30 pairs nesting in Scotland. They are being monitored by the RSPB and Scottish Natural Heritage as part of a five-year programme to reintroduce the bird after it was wiped out around the turn of the century.

P8 Stuart Housden, director of RSPB Scotland, said: 'This is a bird which is very susceptible to poisoning because it's a scavenger by nature. We've put all this time, money and effort into reintroducing it and got cooperation from the Swedish and German governments. It's costing about £50,000 a year to run the programme and yet the birds are still being poisoned and those are only the ones we find or which get reported.'

P9 The report concludes that all the incidents it investigated were almost entirely related to game

Passage G1 (continued)

shooting areas. Gamekeepers this year denied suggestions that they had been solely responsible for the spate of poisonings that had killed birds of prey.

P10 Housden added that the RSPB would be calling on Scottish Environment Minister Lord Sewel to support the campaign against the misuse of poisons. 'We think the misuse of poisons is a very serious underlying problem because it kills indiscriminately. It can affect domestic animals and it's a danger to humans.'

P11 Chief Inspector Cathal MacAskill of Northern Constabulary said: 'The protection of wildlife is one of our key priorities now and we regularly have meetings with estate owners, rangers and gamekeepers to raise the awareness of this issue and the law against it. The welfare of wildlife is important to the wellbeing of the people and the economy of the Highlands and that is why we have a particular focus on it.'

P12 Brian Etheridge, the RSPB's hen harrier specialist, said: 'Too many sheep and deer are stripping Scotland of its heather, and financial support to reintroduce heather moorland to replace grassy fields will help immensely and halt the threat to the hen harrier. However, while the discussions on how best to improve heather moorland management go on – the killing continues.'

Scotland on Sunday, 14 June 1998, © David Love Press Agency

Questions on passage G1 – Fears as numbers of hen harriers plummet

Questions 1 and 2(a) deal with how the passage has been put together, i.e. its structure.

1.   Paragraph 1 states the main point of the article. What is it?

2.   (a) Paragraphs 3–6 provide an explanation as to why this has occurred. Explain the problem.

      (b) Can you explain how the writer has structured the passage up to this point?

3.   (a) Look at paragraphs 7 and 8. Why is poisoning an effective way of killing red kites?

      (b) How does paragraph 7 develop the structure?

4.   (a) Paragraphs 10, 11 and 12 are all quotations from people concerned with the issue. They each have a different focus. Explain the point each person is trying to make. (Use your own words.)

      Paragraph 10. Stuart Housden is saying …

      Paragraph 11. Chief Inspector Cathal MacAskill is saying …

      Paragraph 12. Brian Etheridge is saying …

      (b) Why have these quotations been used?

Passage G2

Highland estate at centre of inquiry

Police raid after bird poison fear

S1 POLICE are investigating the alleged slaughter of birds of prey on the Highland estate of a former magistrate.

S2 Both live and dead birds of prey, including buzzards, were seized in an early-morning raid on the 4000-acre Corrybrough Estate at Tomatin, near Inverness, owned by 56-year-old John Tinsley.

A Northern Constabulary spokeswoman confirmed yesterday a report on the seizures would be sent to the procurator-fiscal.

Mr Tinsley spent two years working as a magistrate in Grantham before concentrating on business commitments. He also has property and farming interests in Lincolnshire.

Police were joined in the raid on Tuesday by officials from the Royal Society for the Protection of Birds and the Scottish Office Agriculture, Fisheries and Environment Department.

The action involving eight officers and officials, was taken under the Wildlife and Countryside Act, which makes it illegal to trap and kill protected birds such as the buzzard.

Ms Elayne Grimes, police press officer, said the operation had been mounted after enquiries which had been going on for some time. She added: 'As a result, a number of birds of prey, both dead and alive, were taken possession of and a report will be forwarded to the procurator-fiscal in Inverness.'

It is believed that among the birds taken from the estate were two buzzards found at a refuse pit. The operation was mounted after an earlier discovery of a dead buzzard and poisoned bait.

An RSPB spokesman confirmed they had assisted in the operation, but declined to comment further.

S3 Neither Mr Tinsley nor his head keeper, Mr Calum Kippen, could be contacted yesterday.

Only last week, Mr Tinsley appeared at Inverness Sheriff Court after denying a number of charges, including failing to stop his vehicle when requested to do so by police, and failing to provide a specimen of breath.

Mr Tinsley has also denied resisting arrest and conducting himself in a disorderly manner and committing a breach of the peace. It was alleged the incidents took place as he left the Tomatin Inn early one morning last October to drive home.

He told the court how he feared the two officers who followed him in an umarked vehicle could have been robbers or kidnappers.

The Corrybrough Estate includes mostly sheep and forestry land, but is also used for sport.

S4 Meanwhile, in Perthshire, one of Scotland's rarest birds of prey is becoming a victim of an illegal poisoning epidemic.

Conservationists were outraged yesterday after a red kite was killed after eating poisoned bait.

It is the third time this year that a red kite has been poisoned and, over the last 12 months, seven of the rare birds have died through poisoning in Scotland. Police yesterday said they are investigating the most recent incident, which came to light when the kite was found dying on farm land in West Strathearn.

The bird, one of a

Passage G2 (continued)

batch of 19 re-introduced to Scotland in 1996, was taken immediately to the vet by the farm manager of the estate, but it died shortly afterwards.

Yesterday Tayside Police wildlife liaison co-ordinator Alan Stewart said that it was totally unacceptable that poisoned baits are still being set in the Scottish countryside.

He said: 'Such baits may well be intended to kill carrion crows, which indeed would readily take them, but they are completely illegal and completely indiscriminate.

'Over the past few years in Tayside, poisoned baits have been responsible for the deaths of dogs, cats, buzzards, owls, peregrine falcons, s p a r r o w h a w k s , hedgehogs, black headed gulls and many more birds and animals.

'This is in fact the second red kite to be killed by poisoned baits in Perthshire in the past year and the third in Scotland this year.'

The RSPB and the kite's death was a devastating loss.

It called for the public to help catch the culprit and for the courts to hand down stiff sentences.

The bird killed was one of 19 from Germany released in the central belt two years ago.

A spokeswoman said: 'It's a devastating blow for a young population trying to establish itself in central Scotland.

'It's extremely unfortunate to find another victim of cruel and indiscriminate poisoning.

'When people are found guilty of these crimes they should be issued with a suitable punishment.

'They are depriving the people of Scotland of a wonderful part of their natural heritage.'

The Herald, 3 April 1998

Questions on passage G2 – Police raid after bird poison fear

1. The passage can be divided into four sections. Read each section separately and decide what is its main point.

   Section 1

   Section 2

   Section 3

   Section 4

   (4)

2. In Section 4 there is a reference to poison. This reference is different from the reference to poison in the previous passage. What is the difference?

   (1)

3. In Section 3, the writer is presenting John Tinsley in a particular way.

   (a) How is he presented?

   (1)

   (b) Which details have been provided to suggest this? Use your own words. We are told that he …

      (i)

      (ii)

   (2)

Passage G3

NEST WATCH DRAMA AS OSPREY EGGS SNATCHED FROM HIGH-RISE HAVEN

S1　IT WAS an operation carried out with military precision. In broad daylight the thieves scaled the 40ft high Scots pine wearing spiked climbing boots to get at the target – an osprey's nest.

Three eggs, due to hatch in less than a fortnight's time, were snatched.

Now security surrounding more than 100 osprey nests has been stepped up following the daring raid in the Highlands.

S2　The theft was discovered at noon on Sunday by Allan Bantick, a local volunteer, who regularly watches the site to guard against intruders.

Mr Bantick, 57, said: 'I was surprised to see that the birds were not on the nest. Then they flew over and looked in. They shuffled about and fidgeted for a while, then flew away again. That is not the behaviour of birds with eggs to look after.'

When he realised what had happened, Mr Bantick called the police, who checked the nest. Yesterday a spokesman for Northern Constabulary said: 'This person must be caught. Often these crimes are committed by a group together, who do not stop at just one nest. They may be stealing to order for a wealthy egg collector and could well strike again.'

S3　The nest has been used since 1982 and last year the same birds successfully raised one healthy chick.

Richard Thaxton, warden at the most famous osprey site at Boat of Garten, Inverness-shire, said yesterday: 'It is a despicable thing to do. The embryos in these eggs were well developed and would have hatched in a very short time.'

Abridged from the *Daily Mail*, 13 May 1997

Questions on passage G3 – Nest watch drama as osprey eggs snatched from high-rise haven

1. Using your own words explain how the egg theft was discovered.

(3)

2. In Section 3 the warden, Richard Thaxton, explains why he thinks the egg theft is despicable.

   (a) What is his reason?

(1)

   (b) What do you think 'despicable' means?

(1)

3. Look back at Section 1.

   (a) Do you think the thieves were well organised?

(1)

   (b) What phrase tells you this?

(1)

Questions on passages G1–G3

1. The three passages have been built in the same way.

   • The headline is first.
   • The main event is in paragraph 1.
   • The detail is developed in the middle of each article
   • There is a quotation at the end.

   Fill in the grid on the next page from the information in all the passages.

Passage	Headlines	Main Point	Detail	Quotations
G1				
G2				
G3				

2. A writer often conveys the point of the writing by very clever use of words. This is his/her craft. Look at the passages you have just read, and decide which one you think shows evidence of real craft.

    (a) Are there phrases or sentences you think very cleverly convey the point of the article? Is it cleverly structured?

    (b) Write a short paragraph on the writer's craft in the passage you think is most cleverly written.

The previous three passages were about birds. The next two passages are on other aspects of the environment and concluding work that draws the close reading work together.

Passage G4
By *Michael McCarthy*

The Otter Makes an Urban Comeback

Once nearly extinct in England, the elusive predator is now returning to old haunts

P1 It is nine minutes past two on an August night and Winchester, a thriving historic city and busy commuter centre, is fast asleep.

P2 One individual in the city centre, however, is very much awake, intent on getting somewhere, and in an old watermill spanning the river Itchen which flows through the city. The individual is suddenly caught by infra-red light and a video camera: a wild otter.

P3 This grainy still is dramatic proof of just how substantial is the otter's comeback. An animal that was extinct in most of England and much of Britain 20 years ago is steadily returning to its former haunts, and swimming right through the middle of conurbations to do so.

P4 Otters have been spotted or traced swimming through Stoke-on-Trent, Reading, Exeter, Glasgow and other urban centres besides Winchester and are present on 28 rivers which flow through towns and cities, according to the most comprehensive account of otter distribution to date, published today by the Wildlife Trusts.

P5 The report, *Splash Back*, shows that because of improvements in water quality and efforts to restore waterside habitats, the otter's gradual recovery has sped up in the past five years. The animals are now recolonising many areas from which they so dramatically disappeared in the late 1950s and 1960s.

P6 The report says otters are at their most numerous in Devon, which has always been their English stronghold, in Scotland and in parts of Wales, but are coming back strongly in East Anglia and in Northumberland – they have been seen three miles from Newcastle upon Tyne. They are spreading from Wales into the Severn and Trent catchment areas and can be found on the edge of Birmingham. Populations are recovering in Wiltshire, Somerset and Hampshire, but Surrey and Kent are largely still awaiting their return.

P7 But the report also sounds warning that otters face new and potentially deadly threats, in the form of pollution, habitat loss and road traffic.

P8 Of particular concern is a family of chemicals used in sheep dips, synthetic pyrethroids (SPs). SPs wipe out aquatic life at the base of the food chain, depriving fish of insect food and leaving otters short of prey: one teaspoon of SP dip/Ω, the report says, could kill the insects in an area the size of an Olympic swimming pool. The Wildlife Trusts are calling for SPs to be withdrawn from sale pending further research.

P9 Loss of habitat is a continuing problem, but death on the roads is also a big threat to otters. Recent research has shown that road traffic kills 60 per cent of the otters that die violently in the UK, so the trusts are calling for measures such as otter underpasses and fencing to become mandatory on all new road, river engineering and rail projects.

P10 'Many animals are very careful about entering a dark tunnel,' said Tim Sykes, the Environment Agency conservationist for Hampshire who is in charge of the otter monitoring at the Winchester mill. 'Sometimes they jump out and walk along the bank. It's a classic problem elsewhere in the country with roads. Otters don't like swimming through a culvert under a road. They would rather walk up the bank and over it. That's when they get killed by traffic.'

P11 The otter pictured scurrying through the Winchester mill had just swum along an open section of the river past footpaths, pubs, private gardens and major roads, until its movement activated the camera. 'Maybe they're not as shy as we used to think,' Mr Sykes said. 'They're just extremely elusive.'

P12 But his study of otters on the Itchen is using something much more ambitious than random photography: DNA fingerprinting of individual otters. Volunteers pick up the otter droppings, or spraints, early in the morning while they are still fresh, and they are sent to Aberdeen University.

P13 It is the first such project of its type in the world, Mr Sykes said. 'Till recently we had to rely on their tracks and signs as clues to their expanding distribution,' he said. 'Using DNA analysis is like moving from the Wright brothers to Neil Armstrong. We should be able to build up a detailed picture of the otter population.'

Splash Back: The Return of the Otter is published by the Wildlife Trusts, The Green, Witham Park, Lincoln LN5 7JR.

An otter caught on video by the River Itchen in the centre of Winchester

Photograph: John Lawrence, *The Independent*

Questions on passage G4 – The otter makes an urban comeback

1.

    (a) Read paragraphs 1, 2 and 3. Paragraphs 1 and 2 are narrative, whereas paragraph 3 is non-fiction. Explain the difference between narrative and non-fiction by referring to these three paragraphs.

        (i)   Paragraph 1 and 2

                                                      (2)

        (ii)   Paragraph 3

                                                      (2)

    (b) What mood are paragraphs 1 and 2 trying to create?

                                                      (1)

    (c) Do you think this kind of writing in the introduction is skilful or silly? Give a reason for your answer.

                                                      (2)

2.   In paragraph 3 the word 'conurbation' appears. Paragraph 4 helps to explain it. What does 'conurbation' mean and how does paragraph 4 explain it?

     'Conurbation' means …

                                                      (1)

     Paragraph 4 tells me this by …

                                                      (1)

3.   Look at paragraph 5. What two reasons are given for the increase in the number of otters?

     (a)

                                                      (1)

     (b)

                                                     (1)

4. What evidence is there to suggest that otters are actually
    spreading from their traditional haunts?

                                                                    (2)

5. Paragraph 7 signals a change in the article. Explain this change.

                                                                    (1)

6. Look at paragraphs 8, 9, 10 and 11. In your own words explain
    the problems otters face.

    (a)
                                                                    (2)

    (b)
                                                                    (2)

    (c)
                                                                    (2)

7. (a) Explain the reference in the last paragraph to Neil Armstrong
        and the Wright brothers.

                                                                    (2)

    (b) How is this tied to the paragraph immediately before it?

                                                                    (2)

Passage and poster G5

LIFESTYLE CHOICES

P5 Personal lifestyle decisions have a major effect on biodiversity, and provide one of the main ways in which individuals can contribute to protecting the biodiversity that is such a simple feature of Scotland and its countryside.

P6 For example, by using cars less and public transport more, and by taking measures to reduce energy wastage at home or in school, we can help reduce the outputs of the fumes that are poisoning the environment and causing 'acid rain' and 'global warming' – the biggest threats of all to biodiversity in Scotland.

P7 Being careful about the chemicals we use in our gardens and selecting environmentally friendly soap powders and washing-up liquids for household use are ways in which we can reduce the poisoning and enrichment of burns and rivers. By avoiding using peat-based composts in the garden or for pot plants, we can help slow the destruction of peat bogs in Scotland and elsewhere in the world. By selecting more recycled products and refusing wastefully packaged products when we shop, by recycling more household wastes, and simply by reducing unnecessary consumption, we can slow the rates at which non-renewable raw materials are stripped from the wild, and reduce the loss of natural habitats under landfill sites and coups.

P1 Every time we switch a light on we increase the demand on power stations, and accelerate their production of waste gases. These gases dissolve in water vapour in the upper atmosphere to create acids, which, when deposited in mist, rain or snow, can damage heather, kill trees or poison fish and other wildlife in rivers or lochs – like this one in Galloway.

BIODIVERSITY CONNECTIONS

acid tests

P2 Although the consequences may not be quite as direct as the poster suggests, the connection between switching on a light and the destruction of heather moorland is a valid one.

P3 Generally in Britain excess electricity demand is met by boosting the output of oil-fired power stations, which increases their production of sulphur dioxide and nitrous oxides as waste gases. Tall chimneys, introduced to minimise local pollution, push these gases high into the atmosphere, where they dissolve in water vapour, forming acids, and are transported long distances before deposition. The acidifying effects of Scottish power stations are felt mostly in Scandinavia, while acid damage in Scotland results mainly from power stations in north-west England.

P4 Research by Aberdeen University has shown that, with increased acidification, the roots of ling heather grow less well, and a recent scientific paper concludes that, as a result, 'the potential for change in the species composition of heather moorland and the Scottish landscape in future years is large'. If heather were to decline, so would the numbers of red grouse and other moorland animals, and so on in turn would the number of golden eagles, thus completing the links in the poster.

biodiversity quotes

'Biodiversity is all living things, from the tiny garden ant to the giant redwood tree. You will find biodiversity everywhere, in window boxes and in wild woods, roadsides and rain forests, snow fields and the sea shore. But don't take plants and animals for granted. We are part of biodiversity and depend on it for our quality of life. And what we don't save now, our children will pay for later.'

From Biodiversity: the UK
Steering Group Report,
HMSO, 1995

Passage and poster G6

biodiversity

TEACHERS NOTES

it's in your hands

> The protection of biodiversity is not just the responsibility of "somebody else". The government, government agencies, local authorities, farmers, foresters, fishermen and voluntary conservation bodies all have an important part to play in biodiversity conservation, but, as this poster emphasises, decisions that each of us makes in our daily lives can also have a damaging or beneficial impact on biodiversity.

> The main objective of lessons based around this set of posters should therefore be to encourage students to think of their own responsibilities for the protection of biodiversity. These Teachers Notes provide further information and ideas to help encourage this process.

SCOTTISH NATURAL HERITAGE

RSPB

A joint venture between Scottish Natural Heritage and the RSPB

Biodiversity publications, Scottish Natural Heritage/RSPB

Questions on passage G5 – Biodiversity

1. Look at paragraph 1. Explain the link between switching on a light and the destruction of rivers. You must use your own words.

    (1)

2. Explain the purpose of paragraph 2.

    (2)

3. Look at paragraphs 3 and 4. What is the connection between power stations and golden eagles?

    (a) Fill in the flow chart below.

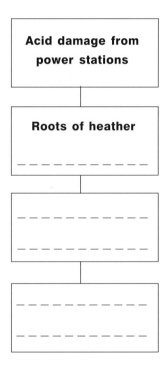

    (4)

    (b) Explain how the poster does in image form what the paragraph has said in words.

    (3)

4.   There is a unifying thread running through these passages on birds, otters and biodiversity. Explain how they are all linked together.

(5)

Reflection

It is easy for people to think that biodiversity only affects people living in the countryside. From your reading of all the passages, what has biodiversity to do with city dwellers and what are their responsibilities?

Summative reading passage (General)

Read the passage below and answer the questions in your own words.

GENETICALLY MODIFIED FOODS – FACTS, WORRIES, POLICIES AND PUBLIC CONFIDENCE
Sir Robert May, Chief Scientific Adviser to the UK Government, considers the issues surrounding GM food (February 1999)

P1 Around the world today, something like 35 million hectares – an area roughly one and a half times the size of Britain – is producing commercial crops of genetically modified (GM) plants. The crops range across soya, maize, oilseed rape, potatoes, cotton and tobacco, and are mostly growing in the USA, Canada and China. The uptake of biotechnology by the agriculture and food sectors in Europe is, by contrast, still at a very early stage though commercial crops of GM maize are growing in Spain and France. No commercial GM crops have been planted in the UK.

P2 This is perhaps surprising. The UK is second only to the USA, and well ahead of other larger countries, in the basic scientific research that is opening new doors in understanding how living things work. From the first recognition of the double helical structure of DNA in Cambridge, to pioneering the sequencing of the genomes of increasingly complicated organisms, the UK has played a disproportionately large role. Our scientists play a major role in developing this science, from basic research into how living organisms work to specific applications, such as cancer research. In particular, in the international collaboration to sequence the human genome – letter by letter to read the instruction manual by which we ourselves are constructed – the UK is doing roughly one third of the work. Furthermore, our pharmaceutical and healthcare industries are among the leaders in beginning to apply this new knowledge to create better drugs, treatments and vaccines, and to think ahead to countermeasures to combat the rising global threat of infections which are multiply resistant to today's antibiotics.

P3 Against this background, why has Europe in general, and the UK in particular, been relatively slow to exploit the new biotechnology in agriculture and foods? And why are so many people so much more worried here than, for example, in the USA?

P4 Part of the answer must, I think, lie in our recent experience with BSE. In essentials, the BSE epidemic among cattle in the 1980s was caused by a rogue prion (a kind of protein, smaller than a virus) whose origins remain unclear: perhaps a rare mutant; perhaps something that has been around for a long time but occurring in so few animals as to escape notice. Whatever its origins, the numbers of animals affected by this prion were hugely amplified by the relatively recent practice of collecting the left-over bits from the abattoir and putting them into the meal fed to their relatives back on the farm. This practice came from an understandable wish for efficiency, making better use of all available protein. In short, BSE in animals and, consequently, new variant CJD in humans, arose as an unintended effect of changing agricultural practice, arguably without sufficiently wide-ranging consultation about the possible consequences. Today it overshadows all discussion of GM foods in the UK, and in Europe more generally.

Genetically modified foods (continued)

P5 Lessons have been learnt. We need to have much better lines of traceability from food production to the table. We should allow consumers maximum information and choice about what they buy through clear labelling. And we must test. No-one was looking out for untoward effects in cattle. In the case of GM food we are testing for unexpected and unwanted effects on human health and on the environment.

P6 So how sure can we be that no nasty surprises lie in wait in GM foods? The worries can be grouped under three broad headings. First, that the genes put into GM foods – the new instructions put into their DNA which effectively tell the plants how to construct themselves – may unwittingly create health hazards for the consumer. I would call this the 'BSE-type' worry. Second, there is the possibility that genes incorporated into a crop to make it resistant to pests or diseases or herbicides may leak out, through cross-pollination or otherwise, into the wider countryside, creating 'superweeds'. By the same token, 'marker genes' are sometimes put in to enable us to identify and keep track of GM plants. Often (and arguably foolishly in my view) these marker genes are antibiotic-resistant, so there could be a risk that humans could acquire these antibiotic-resistance genes from their food, thus accelerating the already existing, and very troublesome, world problem of increasing resistance to today's antibiotics. I would call this worry about unintended consequences elsewhere in the food chain the 'DDT-type' worry. Third, the motivating idea in many GM crops is that no weeds, wildflowers, insects or birds should be able to compete with or consume them. This is an understandable goal from the narrow view of producing food for humans.

P7 But it is bad news for biological diversity in the countryside. In other words, many GM crops will intensify and accelerate changes in the countryside which already exist and which trouble many of us, including me. So I could call these concerns 'hedgerow-type' worries.

Summative reading assessment (General)

Section A – Understanding

1. In paragraph 1 we are told that GM foods are not grown everywhere in the world. Where are the largest areas producing commercial crops of GM plants?

    (2)

2. From paragraph 2, why is it surprising that there are no GM crops planted in the UK?

    (3)

3. (a) In paragraph 4, one cause of BSE is explained. In your own words explain how BSE has occurred.

    (2)

    (b) Was there much research done into the possible consequences of the change in agricultural practice that caused BSE? How do you know?

    (2)

4. (a) In paragraph 5 we are told of the lessons that have been learned as a result of the BSE crisis. What are they?

    (3)

    (b) Explain the link being put forward between BSE and GM food.

    (2)

5. Look at paragraph 6. Explain in your own words the three worries the writer defines for GM foods.

    (3)

    ———
    17

Section B – Analysis

6.   Explain the role of sentence 1 in paragraph 2. 'This is perhaps surprising.'

(2)

7.   (a) In paragraph 2, the writer inserts the phrase 'such as cancer research'. Can you suggest a reason why?

(2)

      (b) He also inserts the words 'letter by letter to read the instruction manual by which we ourselves are constructed' in parenthesis. Why has he added this in?

(2)

8.   Explain the role of paragraph 3 in the argument of the passage.

(2)

9.   In paragraph 5, the writer uses the word 'traceability'. What does it mean and what words in the passage help you to understand it?

(2)

10.   Comment on the sentence 'And we must test' in paragraph 5.

(3)

——
13

Section C – Evaluation

11.　(a)　What is the purpose of this passage?

(1)

(b) For whom is it intended?

(1)

(c) Give evidence from both content and style to support your
answer to (b).

(2)

12.　(a)　What is the main point the writer is making?

(2)

(b) Explain how you know, with reference to content and style.

(2)

13.　How well has the writer conveyed his point of view?

(2)
___
10

Total 40

Credit reading passages

The first four passages are about birds and the questions require pupils to:
- read with understanding
- answer questions on vocabulary
- follow the structure of the passage
- comment on the argument of the four passages as a unit
- comment on the writers' craft.

The remaining passage deals with biodiversity and requires pupils to understand:
- different writing styles
- juxtaposition of words and images
- how an idea can be sustained in a different writing style.

This can be extended by using the 'report' passages and the 'discussion' passages.

These passages are not designed as a series of silent writing tests, but as formative devices in teaching close reading and understanding of the writer's craft. The early passages are best tackled in groups, or teacher led, and the later passages could be written.

The passages range in difficulty – this is deliberate as it allows teachers to select passages at the appropriate level for their pupils. Some pupils may be barely Credit, while others are virtually Higher. The questions are Credit style, and therefore valid as teaching tools.

Passage C1

Grouse disaster sets RSPB a life-or-death dilemma

By Magnus Linklater

P1   As guns are loaded and Barbours donned this morning for what is likely to prove a modest grouse season, the RSPB is facing an agonising dilemma over whether to support the slaughter of hawks and harriers to protect the game birds they prey on.

P2   The society's policy on shooting is strictly neutral, but it has always held that if sporting guns were stilled and nature allowed to take its course, a balance would be struck between gamebirds and predators with both species flourishing.

P3   Now that theory is being put to the test in an experiment at Langholm in Dumfriesshire. Although no one involved is yet prepared to discuss it publicly, it is an open secret that game birds have suffered a catastrophic decline on the moor – which once had the most grouse in Britain – since gamekeepers stopped trying to control birds of prey five years ago. Other species, such as curlew, plover and some small heathland birds, have virtually disappeared.

P4   The hands-off experiment on the Duke of Buccleuch's 25,000-acre estate, now in its final year, has been part-funded by the RSPB, which is monitoring the findings.

P5   Until it was launched, gamekeepers controlled the predators, although they were prevented by law from shooting or poisoning them. Now they stand back as buzzards, hawks and hen harriers, hunting in pairs, take their toll. The result, in their view, has been nothing short of a disaster. Some local landowners believe the moor may never recover.

P6   The Langholm report, which is expected to be drawn up later this year, will come at a point when grouse shooting faces a crisis. Last week, figures produced by the Scottish Landowners' Federation (SLF) showed that since 1977 stocks of grouse have crashed.

P7   Although this season suggests a mild recovery, the prospects are bleak for landowners who need large numbers of birds to attract the big-spending shooting clients they need to make ends meet.

P8   The SLF estimated that in 1994 revenues from grouse shooting brought in only £3 million in Scotland against expenditure of £13.7 million. At least 100 moors have gone out of commission in the past five years, with the loss of about 400 jobs.

P9   The RSPB may well argue that helping landowners to build up stocks of grouse is not its business. But it will find it hard to dispute the findings of a survey in which it has taken part. And if they reveal the loss of other birds, such as larks, curlew and plover, it may have to take action.

P10   Last weekend, David Minns, RSPB head of public affairs for Scotland, said he could not discuss the Langholm experiment. However, he pointed out that on the society's own 32,000-acre estate at Abernethy, where the preservation of black grouse and capercaillie has been the main objective, they have achieved significant increases in numbers without any control of birds of prey – though they have had to shoot foxes and crows, and cull deer.

P11   'The answer lies in having a far greater variety of vegetation than you would see on a traditional grouse moor,' he said. 'If you have trees and scrub, it gives the grouse somewhere to hide and more to feed on.'

The Times, 12 August 1996; © The Times Limited 1996, London

Questions on passage C1 – Grouse disaster sets RSPB a life-or-death dilemma

1.   Read paragraph 1. Explain the dilemma of the RSPB (Royal Society for the Protection of Birds).

2.   Look at the phrase 'Barbour donned' in paragraph 1.

     (a) Suggest what point the writer might be making in using this phrase.

     (b) Why do you think the writer uses this phrase?

3.   Look at paragraph 2. What argument has the RSPB maintained on bird population?

4.   (a) The experiment at the Duke of Buccleuch's estate has had an unexpected result. What is it?

     (b) Which sentence indicates the extent of the damage?

5.   The decrease in grouse has had economic results. What are they?

     (a)

     (b)

6.   In the last two paragraphs the head of the RSPB puts forward a different point of view from the rest of the passage. Using your own words, explain what it is.

7.   How has this passage been structured?

     (a) Identify the main point of each paragraph.

     (b) How is each point led into the next?

     (c) How is the whole passage moved to a conclusion?

Passage C2

FEATHERED ENEMIES
The RSPB should reconsider its position on predators

P1   As the guns blaze out their annual paean to the Glorious Twelfth today, a dispute has broken out on the fringes of the grouse moors that is every bit as fiery and cacophonous. A five-year experiment conducted on a Scottish moor by the Duke of Buccleuch, and the Royal Society for the Protection of Birds, has produced awkward findings for many conservationists. It found that a ban on the shooting of birds of prey allowed their numbers so to increase that they not only decimated thriving colonies of game birds, but also led to catastrophic falls in other protected species.

P2   The experiment at Langholm was the culmination of a movement among bird-lovers and conservationists to stop gamekeepers culling predators such as peregrine falcons, hen harriers and sparrow hawks. These beautiful birds, whose historic associations, elegance in flight and fierce magnificence have entranced generations of Britons were in sharp decline. In recent years, however, a concerted attempt has been made to boost their numbers, protect their habitat and foster their breeding habits. The experiment, on 25,000 acres of moorland, was intended to show that, unmolested by man, birdlife will find a natural balance.

P3   The results are a terrible disappointment for the predator-protectors. Rare heathland birds such as golden plover and curlew were hunted almost to extinction by their feathered enemies. Grouse numbers on what was once one of Scotland's finest estates have fallen so steeply that they may never recover. The local economy is threatened. The Duke of Buccleuch – whose forbearance made the experiment possible – may now feel justified in calling for an immediate curb on the predators, and the RSPB will find powerful arguments opposing its long-held call for man to allow nature to take its course.

P4   Several conclusions seem inevitable. The first is that in an island so crowded where natural conditions have for centuries been distorted by man, it is unrealistic now to adopt a hands-off approach to all species. Where predators are reintroduced, even the sea eagles of western Scotland, they may only be able to be brought back in limited numbers if they are not to upset the balance enjoyed by man.

P5   The second conclusion is that anything that reduces game stock so drastically is bound to run into the opposition of landowners and field sportsmen. Thirdly, conservationists should recognise that birds of prey are probably more able to survive in today's environment than their prey. Peregrines have been found nesting in city centres, and hawks can forage for carrion on motorways. It is the weaker birds that deserve protection, including game birds such as the grey partridge whose numbers are falling despite the fine efforts of the Game Conservancy Trust. The RSPB should look at the Langholm findings and ask whether its absolutist stand is till tenable.

"A disappointing shoot, I only managed to bag a brace"

The Times, 2 August 1996; © The Times Limited 1996, London; Cartoonist: Pugh

Questions on passage C2 – Feathered enemies

1.	The article develops the argument of the previous article in a number of ways. In your own words explain what they are. Look particularly at paragraphs 4 and 5.

	(a) What point is the writer making in paragraph 4?

	(b) In paragraph 5 there are two points being suggested. They are:

		(i)

		(ii)

2.	Look at paragraph 3. Comment on 'predator–protectors'.

3.	Look at the headlines of passages C1 and C2. Which headline do you find more effective? Give a reason for your choice.

Passage C3

Golf club to have crows shot in pursuit of birdie

P1 It may seem excessive, but members of an exclusive Scottish golf club have decided they have had enough – ball thieves will be shot, they have declared.

P2 The policy has been adopted following the growing frustration of players who have found that perfect drive or chip shot come to nothing because flocks of crows are stealing golf balls on the fairways of Prestonfield Golf Club in increasing numbers.

P3 Tomorrow play at the club will be halted to allow professional hunters to shoot hundreds of the birds to rid the club of what members say is the cause of many ruined rounds of golf.

P4 However, whether the surviving crows will learn not to disrupt an Edinburgh man's game of golf is disputed by some members and bird groups who fail to see what can be gained from it.

P5 A member of the club, which has an annual membership of 800 and an annual fee of £385, said that he disagreed with shooting the crows because it would not stop other crows flying into the area. He added: 'It's a case of people who can't shoot birdies shooting crows instead and there is no need for it.'

P6 A spokesman for the Royal Society for the Protection of Birds said that mischievous crows were a common problems for golfers.

P7 He said: 'It's curiosity more than anything else. They see these odd round things and they want to find out what they are.

P8 'It's just one of those things. Shooting crows will not make a difference because more will soon take their place. I have never heard of anything like it.'

P9 Unfortunately for the carrion birds, the normally vociferous animal rights groups fall silent at the mass slaughter of mischievous crows. Crows are considered vermin and the law offers no protection to them.

P10 Inspector Mike Flynn of the Scottish Society for the Protection of Animals said that they would get involved only if the crows were not killed humanely.

P11 According to a poster on the club notice board the 18-hole course will be closed tomorrow, 'to deal with the crow problem'.

P12 Alan Robertson, the secretary of the club, which is next to a wildlife reserve by Duddingston Loch, explained the need for tough measures: 'The crows just swoop down and grab them from any part of the course and if you have just hit a shot of 100 yards there is nothing you can do about it. They then fly away to bury them or drop them in the burn.

P13 'We have tried to discourage them using decoy ping-pong balls covered in mustard but that only worked for a short while and then the crows went back to their old tricks. We have been given the go-ahead to shoot them by the police.

P14 But an official at the Royal and Ancient Club, St Andrews, which governs the rules of golf, said that that there were other ways of dealing with the problem of crows.

P15 He said: 'When a crow or outside agency as we put it takes the ball the golfer can either reposition the ball at the spot where it last was or replace the ball if it has been stolen and the golfer should receive no penalty.'

The Scotsman, 10 December 1997

Questions on passage C3 – Golf club to have crows shot in pursuit of birdie

1.   The article begins in an unusual way for a news story. Explain what is unusual about the opening sentence.

(2)

2.   Paragraph 2 explains the situation. Look at paragraphs 3 to the end of the passage and explain the structure of the article. To do this, divide it into sections, identify the paragraphs in each section and write down the point of each section.

                        Paragraph   Point
        Section 1

        Section 2

        Section 3

        You should now be able to write a summary of how the passage has been put together. Give examples to support your point of view.

(3)

3.   (a) Comment on the tone of the passage.

(1)

        (b) What does the quotation in paragraph 5 contribute to the tone?

(2)

Passage C4

Why *not* shoot them?

There are now several bird species causing havoc in both town and country – yet all are protected. Is that wise or fair, asks *Greg Neale*.

P1 To most nature enthusiasts, cormorants, seals, magpies and other creatures are delightful things to watch. But not everyone sees it that way.

P2 Last week a row that has been simmering along Britain's riverbanks came to the boil. Angry anglers who complain that cormorants are eating 'their' fish have begun to take the law into their own hands. Some fishery owners are having the birds shot or poisoned.

P3 Off the Scottish coast, commercial fishermen are calling for seal culls. Sea eagles are blamed for taking fish from salmon farms. And on the grouse moors, keepers are accused of poisoning the hen harriers they say are threatening their birds.

P4 Wild about wildlife? They certainly are.

P5 In towns and cities, as we become aware of the dwindling voices of some of our most loved songbirds, the raucous predators that prey on them, the magpies and crows, are multiplying.

P6 Does protected status upset the balance of nature? And have some of our most respected nature conservation groups – like the Royal Society for the Protection of Birds – become an over-powerful new orthodoxy?

P7 Conservationist reaction to anglers shooting cormorants was immediate. 'Calls to change the law are premature and calls to break the law are irresponsible,' said Robin Wynde, policy officer for the RSPB.

P8 It is not the first time the conservationists have found themselves in the firing line. In southern England, animal welfare groups have opposed moves to cull the fast-expanding population of Canada geese, accused of consuming crops, and reducing parks to muddy wastes.

P9 And when scientists proposed culling the North American immigrant, the ruddy duck, which they believe threatens to interbreed the European white-headed duck out of existence, there was a similar outcry.

P10 The RSPB was also criticised after it joined police in abortive raids on gamekeepers' homes last month, over inquiries into the suspected poisoning of birds of prey. It emerged then that the society keeps a secret computer database, which it makes available to police, on individuals suspected of killing protected birds, but which also contains uncorroborated accusations.

P11 For some critics, the RSPB has become an unaccountable power, and the criticism does not come solely from the fishing and shooting fraternity.

P12 Attitudes, as well as the balance of nature, are changing in suburban gardens. Latest figures suggest that carrion crow numbers have increased by 151 per cent and magpies by 131 per cent in the last 25 years.

P13 'These birds are being turned into complete menaces: their liking of eggs and young is helping to decimate the songbird population,' Robin Page, the farmer, broadcaster and conservationist, said when the figures were published.

P14 While the influence of conservation groups has increased, the picture of conservation gone mad does not stand up to a closer scrutiny.

P15 'Certainly cormorant numbers have increased in recent years, but what has also happened is a shift over the past two decades from the bird being one that wintered on the coast to some 45 per cent or so wintering inland,' Mr Wynde explained yesterday. 'The reasons for that are not clear'.

P16 'Cormorants have been protected since the 1981 Wildlife and Countryside Act. But we have also seen a marked increase in their suitable feeding habitats inland – especially reservoirs and flooded gravel pits stocked with high concentrations of fish.'

Passage C4 (continued)

P17   The RSPB also points out the danger in assuming that falling catches can be blamed on cormorants. 'A study of Loch Leven, in Scotland, showed catches declining as cormorant numbers increased – but subsequently shooting a large number didn't help,' Mr Wynde pointed out.

P18   'Nutrient run-off from the surrounding countryside had increased, water-weed cover had changed, and so had perch populations and controls on pike.

P19   'Fisheries are very complex; unless you correctly identify the cause of the problem you could spend a lot of time and money ineffectively.'

P20   The increase in magpies and crows also reflects our own irrationalities.

P21   If town councils give a lower priority to magpie management it is not simply because the bird has protected status. It is partly because urban nature lovers – as voters, not to be ignored – are throwing out more rubbish, more bird food, and creating the circumstances for the predators to flourish to the detriment of weaker species.

P22   Scientists also caution against knee-jerk reactions. 'Most bird populations are going to be regulated by their habitat and fluctuate over time,' Mr Wynde said.

P23   'And when there is an absence of clear evidence that they are causing damage on a national scale, it is inappropriate to cull whole populations.

P24   'There are still only some 7,200 breeding pairs of cormorants in this country – and when we turn to hen harriers on grouse moors, where we have under 550 breeding pairs, to shoot them is simply not sustainable.'

P25   Nor should it be forgotten that conservation groups have been struggling for many years against a general assault on nature that is continuing.

P26   Post-war farming practices, the intensive use of pesticides and grubbing up of hedges have all led to the decline of some bird species. Song birds are as much the victim of the spread of the car and its intrusiveness as they are of magpies.

P27   What the story of the cormorants, the magpies, the crows and all the other birds tells us is as revealing as any Aesop fable. When we look at any 'distortion' of nature, we see ourselves, our fashions and our handiwork reflected in the glass.

The Sunday Telegraph, 8 December 1996; © Telegraph Group Limited, 2000

Questions on passage C4 – Why *not* shoot them?

1. In this article the RSPB is criticised for a number of issues. What are they?

   (a)

   (b)

   (2)

2. At the paragraph beginning 'While the influence' (paragraph 14) the article takes a different line of argument.

   (a) Explain the difference.

   (2)

   (b) Which words indicate this shift?

   (2)

3. From the last third of the passage identify the examples of behaviour by humans that are causing problems in the bird population.

   (a)

   (b)

   (c)

   (d)

   (4)

4. (a) Greg Neale asks the question whether it is wise or fair to protect birds that are causing havoc. What is his answer? Look carefully at how the passage is structured and how it moves to a conclusion.

   (2)

   (b) Explain why you have reached this point of view.

   (2)

Questions on passages C1–C4

1. The articles on birds have a common thread, but many differences. Explain, with examples, the similarities and the differences.

    Similarities

    Differences

    (6)

    (6)

2. Look over all the passages you have tackled. There are questions on:
    *   structure
    *   tone
    *   style
    as well as on meaning.

    Decide which passage, or sections of passages, you like best, not for their content, but for the skill of the writer's craft in how they have been structured, or the words the author has chosen.

    Write a short paragraph evaluating the craft of the pieces you have chosen.

Passage C5 – Biodiversity

- The panel of Scientists who compiled Global Biodiversity Assessment made an attempt to assess the number of species in the world (although remember this is only one component of biodiversity).
- About 1.75 million species have been studied by scientists and given scientific names, but many more await scientific discovery. The "best guess" of the scientists who compiled the book was that there are between 13 and 14 million species in the world (although some estimates suggest there may be over 100 million). The most abundant animals were insects (with some 8 million species), while there were estimated to be about 1 million bacteria and 1 ° million fungi. The vertebrates that we know best (including fish, amphibians, reptiles, birds and mammals) had only about 50,000 species.
- Scottish Natural Heritage has attempted recently to quantify the number of species in Scotland, and concluded that about 50,000 species live on the land and in freshwater and another 39,000 species in the seas around Scotland. The pie chart shows how these 89,000 species are divided up amongst the different groups, with the simple protozoan animals being the commonest (37,500 species), followed by the insects (14,000 species).

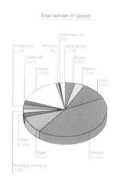

P1 This poster shows that biodiversity covers the whole range of living organisms. The scarce Scots Primrose *(Primula scotia)* often grows no more than 2-4 centimetres tall in the windswept, clifftop grasslands of Orkney, Caithness and Sutherland. It is found nowhere else in the world, making it a unique component of Scotland's biodiversity. The humpback whale can reach 15 metres long. It lives in oceans round the world, and is occasionally seen in waters around Scotland.

Sea cliffs, west coast, Orkney.
Richard Welsby

what is biodiversity?

- Biodiversity (short for 'biological diversity') can be loosely translated as "the total variation in all living things on Earth". This includes not just the total number of species, but also the genetic variation within these species, and the variability of the natural living systems (ecosystems) in which they live.
- The 'official' definition, used in the Biodiversity Convention and adopted by the UK government, states:-
- "'Biological diversity' means the variability among living organisms from all sources, including, inter alia, terrestrial, marine and other aquatic ecosystems and the ecological complexes of which they are part; this includes diversity within species, between species and of ecosystems."
- The definitive book on the subject, called *The Global Biodiversity Assessment* (Heywood, V.H. (Ed), 1995) goes on to explain a bit more about what biodiversity can include:-
- "Were life to occur on other planets, or living organisms to be rescued from fossils preserved millions of years ago, the concept [of biodiversity] could include these as well. It can be partitioned, so that we can talk of the biodiversity of a country, of an area, or of an ecosystem, of a group of organisms, or within a single species."

biodiversity quotes

- *"Biological diversity… is the key to the maintenance of the world as we know it. This is the assembly of life that took a billion years to evolve.*
  It… created the world that creates us. It holds the world steady."
  Edward O. Wilson, *The Diversity of Life*
  (1992)
- *"Great variety in the natural world is easy to take for granted. Yet its stewardship represents a huge responsibility for us all. It is a vivid test of our ability to deliver sustainable development – growth without cheating on our children."*
  John Gummer, Secretary of State for the Environment, November 1996

Biodiversity publication, *The Variety of Life*, Scottish Natural Heritage/RSPB

Questions on passage C5 – Biodiversity

1.   Explain the purpose of this publication.

(2)

2.   Explain how it links with the previous four passages.

(2)

3.   Comment on the structure of the language of this publication.

(2)

Summative reading assessment (Credit)

Read the passage below and answer the questions in your own words.

GENETICALLY MODIFIED FOODS
FACTS, WORRIES, POLICIES AND PUBLIC CONFIDENCE

Sir Robert May, Chief Scientific Adviser to the UK Government, considers the issues surrounding GM food (February 1999)

P1   Around the world today, something like 35 million hectares – an area roughly one and a half times the size of Britain – is producing commercial crops of genetically modified (GM) plants. The crops range across soya, maize, oilseed rape, potatoes, cotton and tobacco, and are mostly growing in the USA, Canada and China. The uptake of biotechnology by the agriculture and food sectors in Europe is, by contrast, still at a very early stage though commercial crops of GM maize are growing in Spain and France. No commercial GM crops have been planted in the UK.

P2   This is perhaps surprising. The UK is second only to the USA, and well ahead of other larger countries, in the basic scientific research that is opening new doors in understanding how living things work. From the first recognition of the double helical structure of DNA in Cambridge, to pioneering the sequencing of the genomes of increasingly complicated organisms, the UK has played a disproportionately large role. Our scientists play a major role in developing this science, from basic research into how living organisms work to specific applications, such as cancer research. In particular, in the international collaboration to sequence the human genome – letter by letter to read the instruction manual by which we ourselves are constructed – the UK is doing roughly one third of the work. Furthermore, our pharmaceutical and healthcare industries are among the leaders in beginning to apply this new knowledge to create better drugs, treatments and vaccines, and to think ahead to countermeasures to combat the rising global threat of infections which are multiply resistant to today's antibiotics.

P3   Against this background, why has Europe in general, and the UK in particular, been relatively slow to exploit the new biotechnology in agriculture and foods? And why are so many people so much more worried here than, for example, in the USA?

P4   Part of the answer must, I think, lie in our recent experience with BSE. In essentials, the BSE epidemic among cattle in the 1980s was caused by a rogue prion (a kind of protein, smaller than a virus) whose origins remain unclear: perhaps a rare mutant; perhaps something that has been around for a long time but occurring in so few animals as to escape notice. Whatever its origins, the numbers of animals affected by this prion were hugely amplified by the relatively recent practice of collecting the left-over bits from the abattoir and putting them into the meal fed to their relatives back on the farm. This practice came from an understandable wish for efficiency, making better use of all available protein. In short, BSE in animals and, consequently, new variant CJD in humans, arose as an unintended effect of changing agricultural practice, arguably without sufficiently wide-ranging consultation about the possible consequences. Today it overshadows all discussion of GM foods in the UK, and in Europe more generally.

Genetically modified foods (continued)

P5 Lessons have been learnt. We need to have much better lines of traceability from food production to the table. We should allow consumers maximum information and choice about what they buy through clear labelling. And we must test. No-one was looking out for untoward effects in cattle. In the case of GM food we are testing for unexpected and unwanted effects on human health and on the environment.

P6 So how sure can we be that no nasty surprises lie in wait in GM foods? The worries can be grouped under three broad headings. First, that the genes put into GM foods – the new instructions put into their DNA which effectively tells the plants how to construct themselves – may unwittingly create health hazards for the consumer. I would call this the 'BSE-type' worry. Second, there is the possibility that genes incorporated into a crop to make it resistant to pests or diseases or herbicides may leak out, through cross-pollination or otherwise, into the wider countryside, creating 'superweeds'. By the same token, 'marker genes' are sometimes put in to enable us to identify and keep track of GM plants. Often (and arguably foolishly in my view) these marker genes are antibiotic-resistant, so there could be a risk that humans could acquire these antibiotic-resistance genes from their food, thus accelerating the already existing, and very troublesome, world problem of increasing resistance to today's antibiotics. I would call this worry about unintended consequences elsewhere in the food chain the 'DDT-type' worry. Third, the motivating idea in many GM crops is that no weeds, wildflowers, insects or birds should be able to compete with or consume them. This is an understandable goal from the narrow view of producing food for humans. But it is bad news for biological diversity in the countryside. In other words, many GM crops will intensify and accelerate changes in the countryside which already exist and which trouble many of us, including me. So I could call these concerns 'hedgerow-type' worries.

P7 I will now consider each of these three categories of worry in turn, and conclude by emphasising – present worries being acknowledged – some of the potential long-term benefits of GM foods.

P8 A fourth kind of worry should be recognised, even though I will not deal with it. This is the argument that says that God did not intend us to meddle with nature in this way. In my view this argument, pursued to its logical conclusion, might see us as still being small, roving bands of hunters and gatherers. But even when we were, we were busy changing our environment, not least in killing off big mammals. Changing circumstances, and our own responses to such change, seem to be built into our history, no matter how you look at it.

Genetic modification – the facts

P9 Genes are the instructions that give organisms their characteristics. These instructions are stored in each cell of every living organism in a long string-like molecule called DNA. The full set of instructions is called a genome. All organisms have genomes of varying sizes; for instance the human genome has an estimated 60–100,000 genes; most plants have about 20,000; the nematode worm (a microscopic creature) has about 18,000; and the single-celled Escherichia coli bacterium has just over 4,000.

P10 Our knowledge of genetics allows the identification of individual genes, and often understanding of their specific properties. The technique of genetic modification (also known as genetic engineering, and genetic manipulation) allows those individual genes to be cut out of the genome of one organism and pasted into the genome of another.

P11 Deoxyribonucleic acid (DNA) is the genetic material of all plants, animals and bacteria and of many viruses. It is made up of just four building blocks called nucleotides (or

Genetically modified foods (continued)

bases) – Adenine (A), Cytosine (C), Guanine (G), and Thymine (T). It is the linear sequence of these bases that contains the genetic information. Rather like Morse Code, only instead of two elements (dots and dashes) the DNA code has four – A, C, G, T. DNA usually exists as two separate strands, twisted together in the well known double helix patterns. The genetic difference between species, and organisms within a species, lies in the different ordering or sequence of these bases and the genes that they form.

P12 In the first genetic modification experiments, which took place in the mid-1970s, synthetic human genes were combined with genes from a bacterium. Many apprehensions of possible dangers were raised at this time. They were carefully addressed by the scientific community (in particular at a noted conference in Asiloman), and none of these conjectured problems have actually arisen. Later that decade, researchers learned how to insert genes into fungi and yeast. In the 1980s they found ways of putting foreign genes into the cells of plants and some animals. In the 1990s the first experiments to insert new genes into human cells and tissues were developed.

P13 In principle, genetic modification allows researchers to move genes between all living creatures. In practice, so far it has only been made to work in a few animal, plant, and microbial species – usually organisms that humans have used for many years in agriculture, food manufacture and industry.

P14 What is perhaps most surprising about genetic modification methods is that they work at all. How is it possible that genes from one organism can be processed by an unrelated organism? The answer lies in the fact that DNA has the same basic characteristics in all organisms. Because all DNA is composed of the same basic ingredients, a gene pasted from, for example, a simple organism like a virus can, in principle, function in the same way in a more complex organism like a plant.

P15 Modern computer databases containing huge amounts of sequence data from large-scale genome projects are making the task of identifying genes with particular desired characteristics (for example the gene that codes for production of vitamin C in citrus fruit) far easier than in the past. Once identified and isolated, gene sequences can be cut and pasted into bacteria, which then manufacture multiple copies of the genes. This enables, for example, the production of essential medicines like insulin to be produced from GM bacteria rather than from animals. Such insulin is produced in a cleaner, more controllable environment than was previously the case. Other sequences are often introduced at this stage, for instance, selective marker genes conferring resistance to one or more antibiotics are often linked to the trait genes to allow researchers to pick out only those bacteria that have successfully received the new gene sequences. Extra regulatory sequences may also be added at this stage, to control the gene's expression, i.e. whether it should function only in certain parts of the new host, or 'switch on' at a certain stage of its development.

P16 Once the gene is complete within the 'carrier', it needs to be inserted into the new host. For GM plants and animals, this stage is complicated by the need to introduce the genes into all the cells in the organism. This can be achieved by inserting the prepared genes into a single cell of the new host. This single cell can then be cultured into a whole organism in which all the cells contain a copy of the introduced gene (the process works similarly if a gene is removed instead of added). A number of methods are used to insert genes into cells. Bacteria and yeasts are often encouraged with chemical and electrical treatments, and disarmed viruses can be used to carry genes into animals, plant and human cells. There are also direct ways of taking genes into cells: by injecting them with very fine needles or by forcing them in aboard tiny metallic bullets. Amazingly, these techniques do not damage the cells.

Summative reading assessment (Credit)

Section A – Understanding

1.   In paragraph 1 we are told that GM foods are not grown everywhere in the world. Where is the largest area producing commercial crops of GM plants?

(2)

2.   From paragraph 2, why is it surprising that there are no GM crops planted in the UK?

(3)

3.   (a) In paragraph 4, one cause of BSE is explained. In your own words explain how BSE has occurred.

(2)

   (b) Was there much research done into the possible consequences of the change in agricultural practice that caused BSE? How do you know?

(2)

4.   (a) In paragraph 5 we are told of the lessons that have been learned as a result of the BSE crisis. What are they?

(3)

   (b) Explain the link being put forward between BSE and GM food.

(2)

5.   Look at paragraph 6. Explain in your own words the three worries the writer defines for GM foods.

(3)

6. What is the argument of paragraph 8 and how does it link to the other arguments?

(2)

7. By looking at the section on 'Genetic modification: the facts' explain genetic modification in your own words.

(2)

8. Trace the development of genetic modification since the 1970s.

(3)

9. Explain the link between GM foods and computer technology.

(2)

———
26

Section B – Analysis

10. Explain the role of sentence 1 in paragraph 2: 'This is perhaps surprising.'

(2)

11. (a) In paragraph 2, the writer inserts the phrase 'such as cancer research'. Can you suggest a reason why?

(2)

    (b) He also inserts the words 'letter by letter to read the instruction manual by which we ourselves are constructed' in parenthesis. Why has he added this?

(2)

12. Explain the role of paragraph 3 in the argument of the passage.

(2)

13. In paragraph 5, the writer uses the words 'traceability'. What does it mean and what words in the passage help you to understand it?

(2)

14. Comment on the sentence 'And we must test' in paragraph 5.

(3)

15.   Look at paragraph 7.

        (a) What is the point of the passage?

        (1)

        (b) If the sentence had ended at the word 'turn' would the passage have had a different point? Give a reason for your answer.

        (2)

16.   Comment on the language of paragraph 8. How does it convey the writer's point of view?

        (2)

17.   Explain, with reference to the text, differences in style between paragraphs 1–8 and the section 'Genetic modification: the facts'.

        (3)

        ___
        21

Section C – Evaluation

18.   (a) What is the purpose of this passage?

        (1)

        (b) For whom is it intended?

        (1)

        (c) Give evidence from both content and style to support your answer to (b).

        (2)

19.   (a) What is the main point the writer is making?

        (2)

        (b) Explain how you know, with reference to content and style.

        (2)

20.   Looking at the passage as a whole, how well has the writer conveyed his point to the reader?

        (5)

        ___
        13

        Total 60

Critical evaluation of literature (CEL)

A lengthy anthology of texts is beyond the remit of this publication. The following sections on prose, poetry, drama and media serve as starting points into the concept of biodiversity in literature.

Prose

Teachers' introduction

Teachers could use the biodiversity material to support teaching a science fiction novel. A text such as *The Day of the Triffids* lends itself ideally to the topic, but there is mileage in any science fiction novel, since much science fiction works as a comment on the lives we are leading at the moment. The power of science fiction rests on extrapolating from our present course of behaviour to its potential consequences.

If a class has studied *The Day of the Triffids*, the teacher could direct pupils to the non-fiction material in this section and the questions that follow.

On the other hand if the class has not studied *The Day of the Triffids*, part of it is reprinted below to lead in to the non-fiction beyond.

As this text is not designed as close reading, no directive questions have been set on the texts.

Many of the questions in the close reading section are preparation for this – questions on tone, craft, structure, etc. The 'Triffids' material and accompanying articles lend themselves to oral work, either teacher led or group discussion.

The newspaper articles could be used in tandem with the Triffids excerpts, as further teaching material on comparative styles on related topics. The extract on page 106 ('The lakes of death bred by rain and sun') could be used with the extract 'Seeds of destruction' on page 177 (Report writing, item G7).

The last story in 'Six Lives of Fankle the Cat' (not reprinted here) by George Mackay Brown is a delightful tale called 'Moon Animals', in which the animals of the moon have to decide what to do with the destructive creature, Man. It would provide a sound listening exercise, as well as a further style of writing and a different slant on the same topic. It also is a short story that could easily be used as a CEL prose.

Prose – fiction

THE COMING OF THE TRIFFIDS

When I was a child we lived, my father, my mother, and myself, in a southern suburb of London. We had a small house which my father supported by conscientious daily attendance at his desk in the Inland Revenue Department, and a small garden at which he worked rather harder during the summer. There was not a lot to distinguish us from the ten or twelve million other people who used to live in and around London in those days.

My father was one of those persons who could add a column of figures with a flick of the eye so that it was natural for him to have in mind that I should become an accountant. As a result, my inability to make any column of figures reach the same total twice caused me to be something of a mystery as well as a disappointment to him. Still, there it was: just one of those things. My father would read my school reports with a gloom which in other respects they scarcely warranted.

'I really don't know what we shall do with you. What do you *want* to do?' he would ask.

And until I was thirteen or fourteen I would shake my head, conscious of my sad inadequacy, and admit that I did not know.

My father would then shake *his* head.

It did not occur to me that the subject which interested me most could lead to a career – and my father failed either to notice, or, if he did, to care that reports on my biology were consistently good.

It was the appearance of the triffids which really decided the matter for us. Indeed, they did a lot more than that for me. They provided me with a job and comfortably supported me. They also on several occasions almost took my life. On the other hand, I have to admit that they preserved it, too, for it was a triffid sting that had landed me in hospital on the critical occasion of the 'comet debris'.

In the books there is quite a lot of loose speculation on the sudden occurrence of the triffids. Most of it is nonsense. Certainly they were not spontaneously generated as many simple souls believed. Nor did most people endorse the theory that they were a kind of sample visitation – harbingers of worse to come if the world did not mend its ways and behave its troublesome self. Nor did their seeds float to us

The Coming of the Triffids (continued)

through space as specimens of the horrid forms life might assume upon other, less favoured worlds – at least, I am satisfied that they did not.

I learned more about it than most people because triffids were my job, and the firm I worked for was intimately, if not very gracefully, concerned in their public appearance. Nevertheless, their true origin still remains obscure. My own belief, for what it is worth, is that they were the outcome of a series of ingenious biological meddlings – and very likely accidental at that.

The world at that time was rather an exciting place – for a biologist anyway. Every year we were pushing the northern limit of growth for food plants a little farther back. New fields were growing quick crops on what had historically been simply tundra or barren land. Every season, too, stretches of desert both old and recent were reclaimed and made to grow grass or food. For food was then our most pressing problem, and the progress of the regeneration schemes and the advance of the cultivation lines on the maps was followed with almost as much attention as an earlier generation had paid to battlefronts.

Meanwhile sustained research in rocketry had at last succeeded in attaining one of its objectives. It had sent a missile with an explosive warhead far enough up for it to fall into an orbit round the earth. Once there it would continue to circle like a tiny moon, quite inactive and innocuous – until the pressure on a control-room button should give it the impulse to drop back, with devastating effect.

Great as was the public concern which followed the triumphant announcement of the first nation to establish a satellite weapon satisfactorily, a still greater concern was felt over the failure of others to make any announcement at all even when they were known to have had similar successes. It was by no means pleasant to realize that there was an unknown number of menaces up there over your head, quietly circling and circling until someone should arrange for them to drop – and that there was nothing to be done about them. Still, life has to go on – and novelty is a wonderfully short-lived thing. One became used to the idea perforce. From time to time there would be a panicky flare-up of expostulation when reports circulated that as well as satellites with atomic heads there were others with such things as crop diseases, cattle diseases, radio-active dusts, viruses, and infections not only of familiar kinds, but brand-new sorts recently thought up in laboratories, all floating around up there.

The Coming of the Triffids (continued)

At this point all parties tacitly gave up denying or confirming anything about satellites, and an intensified effort was made to divert the public interest back again to the no less important, but far less acrimonious, matter of food scarcity.

Nonetheless hardly anyone heard of even the existence of Umberto Christoforo Palanguez. I only heard of him myself years later in the course of my work.

Umberto was of assorted Latin descent, and something South American by nationality. His first appearance occurred when he walked into the offices of the Arctic and European Fish-Oil Company, and produced a bottle of pale pink oil in which he proposed to interest them.

Arctic and European displayed no eagerness. The trade was pretty well tied up. However, they did in the course of time get around to analysing the sample he had left with them.

The first thing they discovered about it was that it was not a fish-oil, anyway: it was a vegetable, though they could not identify the source. The second revelation was that it made most of their best fish-oils look like grease-box fillers. Alarmed, they sent out what remained of the sample for intensive study and put round hurried inquiries to know if Mr Palanguez had made other approaches.

When Umberto called again the managing director received him with flattering attention.

'That is a very remarkable oil you brought us, Mr Palanguez,' he said.

Umberto nodded his sleek, dark head. He was well aware of the fact.

'I have never seen anything quite like it,' the managing director admitted.

Umberto nodded his head again.

'No?' he said politely. Then, seemingly as an afterthought, he added: 'But I think you will, senor. A very great deal of it.' He appeared to ponder. 'It will, I think, come on the market, seven, maybe eight, years from now.' He smiled.

The Coming of the Triffids (continued)

'H'm,' said the managing director. 'Well, I suppose you have a proposition, Mr Palanguez. Shall we come to it?'

'I think,' Umberto told him, 'I think that I might be able to supply you with seeds of this plant in, maybe, six months time. If you were to plant then you could begin production of oil in five years – or it might be six for full yield.'

'I see. Now what was the figure you had in mind for getting us the seeds of this thing?'

Umberto named a sum which stopped the managing director's doodling quite abruptly. It made him take off his glasses to regard the speaker more closely. Umberto was unabashed.

'Consider, señor,' he said, ticking off points on his fingers. 'It is difficult. And it is dangerous – very dangerous. I do not fear – but I do not go to danger to amuse myself. There is another man, a Russian. I shall have to bring him away, and he must be paid well. There will be others that he must pay first. Also I must buy an aeroplane – a jet aeroplane, very fast. All these things cost money.'

'And I tell you it is not easy. You must have seeds that are good. Many of the seeds of this plant are infertile. To make sure, I have to bring you seeds that have been sorted. They are valuable. And in Russia everything is a state secret and guarded. Certainly it will not be easy.'

'It will need thinking over, Mr Palanguez.'

'But of course, señor!' Umberto agreed, with a smile. 'I can wait – a little while. But I'm afraid I cannot reduce my price.'

Nor did he.

He got his agreement, for his samples were convincing, if the rest was somewhat vague.

In point of fact it cost those interested quite a lot less than they had undertaken to pay, for after Umberto went off with his aeroplane and his advance he was never seen again. What happened to him will never be definitely known. It is my guess that over the Pacific Ocean somewhere high up in the stratosphere, he and his companion found themselves being attacked. It may be that the first they knew of it was

The Coming of the Triffids (continued)

when cannon-shells from Russian fighters started to break up their craft.

And I think, too, that one of those shells blew to pieces a certain twelve-inch cube of plywood – the receptacle like a small tea-chest in which the triffid seeds were packed.

Perhaps Umberto's plane exploded, perhaps it just fell to pieces. Whichever it was, I am sure that when the fragments began their long, long fall towards the sea they left behind them something which looked at first like a white vapour.

It was not vapour. It was a cloud of seeds, floating, so infinitely light they were, even in the rarefied air. Millions of gossamer-slung triffid seeds, free now to drift wherever the winds of the world should take them…

It might be weeks, perhaps months, before they would sink to earth at last, many of them thousands of miles from their starting place.

That is, I repeat, conjecture. But I cannot see a more probable way in which that plant, intended to be kept a secret, could come, quite suddenly, to be found in almost every part of the world.

My introduction to a triffid came early. It so happened that we had one of the first in the locality growing in our own garden. The plant was quite well developed before any of us bothered to notice it, for it had taken root along with a number of other casuals behind the bit of hedge that screened the rubbish heap. It wasn't doing any harm there, and it wasn't in anyone's way. So when we did notice it later on we'd just take a look at it now and then to see how it was getting along, and let it be.

However, a triffid is certainly distinctive, and we couldn't help getting a bit curious about it after a time. Not, perhaps, very actively, for there are always a few unfamiliar things that somehow or other manage to lodge in the neglected corners of a garden, but enough to mention to one another that it was beginning to look a pretty queer sort of thing.

Nowadays when everyone knows only too well what a triffid looks like it is difficult to recall how odd and somehow *foreign* the first ones appeared to us. Nobody, as far as I know, felt any misgiving or alarm

The Coming of the Triffids (continued)

about them then. I imagine that most people thought of them – when they thought of them at all – in much the same way that my father did.

I have a picture in my memory of him examining ours and puzzling over it at a time when it must have been about a year old. In almost every detail it was a half-size replica of a fully-grown triffid – only it didn't have a name yet, and no one had seen one fully grown. My father leant over, peering at it through his horn-rimmed glasses, fingering its stalk, and blowing gently through his gingery moustache as was his habit when he was thoughtful. He inspected the straight stem, and the woody bole from which it sprang. He gave curious, if not very penetrative, attention to the three small, bare sticks which grew straight up beside the stem. He smoothed the short sprays of leathery green leaves between his finger and thumb as if their texture might tell him something. Then he peered into the curious, funnel-like formation at the top of the stem, still puffing reflectively but inconclusively through his moustache. I remember the first time he lifted me up to look inside that conical cup and see the tightly-wrapped whorl within. It looked not unlike the new, close-rolled frond of a fern, emerging a couple of inches from a sticky mess in the base of the cup. I did not touch it but I knew the stuff must be sticky because there were flies and other small insects struggling in it.

More than once my father ruminated that it was pretty queer, and observed that one of these days he really must try to find out what it was. I don't think he ever made the effort, nor, at that stage, was he likely to have learned much if he had tried.

The thing would be about four feet high then. There must have been plenty of them about, growing up quietly and inoffensively, with nobody taking any particular notice of them. At least it seemed so, for if the biological or botanical experts were excited over them no news of their interest percolated to the general public. And so did thousands like it in neglected spots all over the world.

It was some little time later that the first one picked up its roots, and walked.

John Wyndham, *The Day of the Triffids*, Hutchison: reference Wyndham/9.6.00/2

Prose – non-fiction

Passage A

The lakes of death bred by rain and sun

Nicholas Schoon

After the flood: The Somerset levels near Curry Rivel where 50 million gallons of rainwater have lain rotting for a month, creating poisonous lakes and killing fish. Scientists have added hydrogen peroxide to reoxygenate the water. Photograph: Marc Hill

Millions of gallons of black and stinking flood-water have caused a farming and ecological disaster on one of Britain's most important and unusual wetlands.

Thousands of fish – bream, pike, roach and others – have been killed by the stagnant deoxygenated water which has covered hundreds of acres of the Somerset Levels for the past month. Rich cattle pastures have been wiped out.

The Government's Environment Agency is using large quantities of hydrogen peroxide, a volatile corrosive chemical, to raise oxygen levels in the floodwater, so that it can be pumped off the fields and into a river without killing more fish.

Exactly a month ago, heavy downpours flooded more than one thousand acres of land. When the rain stopped and the sun shone, the temperature climbed and bacteria began to rot the lush grass and cattle dung lying below the surface.

The microbes consumed most of the oxygen dissolved in the water within a few days. The decomposition turned the water black, produced a foul stench and killed the abundant fish, snails and water insects living in the network of ditches and dikes which drain the levels.

First the Environment Agency tried pumping the water into nearby rivers, which just killed more fish. Then they bubbled fresh oxygen through the water, which was simply too large a task – there are 50 million gallons of water after all.

Their last hope was hydrogen peroxide. This corrosive chemical, more normally used as hair bleach, adds free oxygen to water. More than sixty tons of the chemical will have been mixed in by the time the task is finished, probably this weekend. Pumping the then fish-friendly water can then begin in earnest.

The levels around Glastonbury and Bridgwater are mostly Government-designated Sites of Special Scientific Interest. These flat pastures are a haven for more than 10,000 ducks and wading birds in winter and spring. There is a rich variety of plants and smaller animals living on the pastures and in the ditches, although parts of the levels are used for intensive cattle farming.

The National Farmers Union said some 50 farmers were affected. 'The more productive grazing and silage fields will have to be ploughed up,' said regional director Anthony Gibson. 'The floodwater was like a rancid soup, stinking to high heaven.'

The water which has already receded has left behind brown, dead, vegetation. 'The moor looks very sick, sad and sorry,' said John Leece, for the Royal Society for the Protection of Birds. Herons have been flocking in to eat all the dead fish. 'There are worries about the vegetation and the fish, but I think the birds are going to be fine,' said Mr Leece.

The Independent, 4 September 1997

Passage B

Winter saved coast from full effects of Sea Empress spill

By Charles Clover, Environment Editor

THE FALL-OUT

- 2,000 tonnes of oil spilled, clean-up bill totalled £100 million.
- 7,000 oiled birds washed ashore. Of 3,000 rescued, 60 per cent lived. Best survival rate: mute swans. Worst: guillemots and red-throated divers.
- 40 per cent of the oil evaporated soon after spill and 52 per cent was broken down by micro-organisms. Only a small amount was stranded on shore.
- A year later, under one per cent remained on coastline – only a tiny amount in a form that could cause long-term problems.

A fortunate combination of factors spared many birds, fish and holiday beaches after the grounding of the Sea Empress oil tanker, a report found yesterday.

The accident on February 15 1996 cost up to £100 million in losses to the tourist trade and bills to clear the 72,000 tons of oil from Milford Haven, Pembrokeshire.

But Professor Ron Edwards, chairman of the Sea Empress Environmental Evaluation Committee, said the pollution would have caused more damage if the ship had run aground in summer. Birds would have been nesting and tourist resorts full.

The spillage was the third largest to hit the British coast. However, it could have been a lot worse, he said. 'We were very fortunate,' he added. 'But that is not to say that it was minimal.

'It happened when the birds were not nesting and the fish were not spawning. The wind was blowing offshore and as a result the oil was largely dispersed. Tourist beaches were not crowded and there was time to clean up before they arrived.'

The findings of the two-year study, the subject of a three-day conference in Cardiff this week, highlight several shortcomings in the way such incidents are handled.

It referred to the amount of time and money spent trying to save sea birds which either did not survive being cleaned or died soon after being released.

A special survey found that more than 70 per cent of guillemots died within 14 days of release and only three per cent survived for two months.

Of the 3,000 birds rescued, 60 per cent lived. The best survival rate was among mute swans, while the worst was among guillemots and red-throated divers.

The study concluded that there was 'no conservation case for cleaning'. It asked whether it was not better to kill some birds humanely when they were found, rather than put them through the stress of cleaning.

The RSPCA, which was largely responsible for collecting and organising the cleaning of the oiled birds, was asked to ensure tougher standards when volunteers were recruited.

There was criticism that some of those who helped the operation were unskilled in handling the birds.

A total of 7,000 oiled birds were washed ashore but many more died at sea. The study said that, two years on, those most affected included the common scoter ducks. The winter after the spill, 10,000 fewer of the ducks visited the area.

At West Angle Bay, across from where the tanker ran aground, the population of rare cushion star was reduced from 150 to 13. The report said the shoreline ecology was recovering, but in sheltered areas recovery might take years.

Many limpets and other molluscs died on heavily oiled shores. This led to a 'green flush' of

Passage B (continued)

algae and weed which they would normally have eaten. Small crustaceans, such as shrimps and sand hoppers were also killed in large numbers. There appeared to be no impact on seals, porpoises and other mammals.

Although oil levels increased in the tissue of some fish species temporarily, very few died.

The report said fish and mammals were able to avoid the worst of the oil and any that they absorbed was probably broken down by their enzyme systems. It said that 40 per cent of the oil evaporated soon after the spill, 52 per cent was broken down by microorganisms and a small amount was stranded on shore.

A year later, less than one per cent remained on the coastline and only a small amount was found in a form that could cause long-term environmental problems.

Tourist beaches, including Tenby, were cleaned up enough to allow holidaymakers to use them at Easter, nine weeks after the spill. The economic effect to tourism was far less than expected.

Though fishing was banned for 810 square miles as a precaution to protect public health, no damage had been found to any major fish stock, including salmon and sea trout. The local fishing industry suffered losses from the ban estimated at £7–12 million.

The report said the clean-up of more than 120 miles of coastline was handled well. The use of chemical dispersants almost certainly reduced the levels of oil on the shore and the number of birds affected at sea.

The committee called for a statutory duty to be placed on all coastal local authorities to have oil spill contingency plans, as Dyfed county council had in this case.

Professor Edwards said Lord Donaldson made a similar recommendation after his inquiry into the Braer disaster, but nothing had been done.

The committee, which was set up by the Government, also said there was a need for the monitoring of wildlife damage to start immediately after a spillage and for better monitoring of wildlife movements.

It suggested that an overall commander be appointed at the scene of a major incident to act as a spokesman.

It also called for compensation for the cost of environmental impact studies to come from the shipping and oil companies responsible.

Calls for a year-round oil watch tug to be stationed in the Western Approaches were rejected yesterday by the transport minister, Glenda Jackson.

Professor Edwards was asked if this was an unwise decision given that a fast-response vessel might have averted the Sea Empress accident. He answered: 'I would have preferred to have the tug.'

Ron Davies, the Secretary of State for Wales, welcomed the report and asked for comments on any of the recommendations.

'I'm pleased that the report shows that the clean-up operation was effective and there appear to have been few major long-term effects,' he said.

However, Friends of the Earth said it was far too early to know how much damage to wildlife had been caused. Gordon James, a spokesman, said: 'Oil can still be found in some of the sheltered bays of Milford Haven. It's too early to know exactly what damage has been done. More studies will have to be carried out.'

The Daily Telegraph, 12 February 1998; © Telegraph Group Limited 2000

Passage C

Thousands of fish die as pollution infests river

By Charles Clover, Environment Editor

A major pollution incident in which at least 150 tons of fish were said to have died on the River Dun, a tributary of the Kennet, near Hungerford, Berks, was being investigated by the Environment Agency last night.

Unknown pollution killed almost all the fish in a trout farm and is reported to have affected the rivers Kennet and Dun and the Kennet and Avon Canal.

The agency said it was one of the largest fish kills from pollution in the Thames Valley for many years.

The alarm was given by William Stephenson, the owner of the Berkshire Trout Farm, Lower Denford, at midnight on Tuesday after he had discovered at least 1,000 dead trout.

Mr Stephenson said: 'Lifting hundreds of dead fish from the water is just dreadful. It breaks my heart. I wish we could find the culprit but the Environmental Agency still don't know who is responsible or what the cause is. The pollution seems to have made its way through the pens housing the fish. The ones that are still alive will have to be culled because they are full of pollutant and couldn't be eaten. It will take me at least two years to recover from this,' he said.

Geoffrey Carhill, of the agency's Thames region, said: 'This is one of the worst cases of pollution in over a decade. Most of the pollution came down the River Dun.'

A rat is reported to have died after eating one of the polluted fish.

The Daily Telegraph, 5 March 1998; © Telegraph Group Limited 2000

Questions on the fiction passage and non-fiction passages A–C

1. Comment on the similarity of content between the fiction passage and the non-fiction passages (A–C).

2. What points are the various writers trying to make?

3. How are they trying to make their point?

   (a) Look closely at the way each passage has been structured.

   (b) Look closely also at the words that have been chosen. (How, for example, are the triffids described? How are the dead fish presented to the reader?)

4. Consider the strengths and weaknesses of each genre as a way of conveying an author's point.

Passage D

Northumberland Wildlife Trust
Garden House, St Nicholas Park
Newcastle Upon Tyne NE3 3XT
Tel: (0191) 284 6884
Fax: (0191) 284 6794
E-mail: mail@northwt.org.uk

10th June 1998

**********News Release**********News Release**********News Release********

500 DAYS TO ENVIRONMENTAL DISASTER

An environmental disaster of international importance is waiting to happen on our doorstep, and Northumberland Wildlife Trust are calling on the Government to do something about it.

Early in the year 2000, heavily polluted minewater from the abandoned Whittle Colliery in Northumberland will spill over into the River Coquet, a Site of Special Scientific Interest, with disastrous consequences for wildlife.

Water levels in the disused shafts at Whittle Colliery are rising at a rate of 10 cm a day, and will soon overtop. A huge quantity of iron hydroxide (together with manganese and other pollutants) will enter the river system at a rate of up to 5000 cubic metres per day. The iron forms a highly visible red deposit on the river bed, which smothers plant life, and in turn has a knock-on effect in the food chain, killing invertebrates and fish.

Initial samples indicate a concentration of 42–1000 mg per litre, which will turn the Coquet and its tributaries, the Tyelaw, Hazon and Swarland Burns, blood-red. A similar incident at Ynysarwed, Wales in 1993, (which had a concentration of only 400 mg/l) had a disastrous effect on the fish populations of the Neath Canal, threatening not only wildlife, but also the fishing and tourism industry.

more follows

INVESTOR IN PEOPLE

Putting *wildlife* on the map

Passage D (continued)

The Coquet is a nationally important river for wildlife, as it contains large populations of salmon, sea and brown trout, and is a spawning ground for marine lampreys. Any pollution would also affect the return of the otter. Drinking supplies to thousands of people are at risk, and the damage to local tourism in the Coquet estuary could be enormous.

David Stewart, Northumberland Wildlife Trust's Chief Executive said: 'This could be a real disaster for the region. The scale and urgency must be recognised and the Government called upon to respond immediately.'

A solution to the problem has been proposed, but at a cost. The Environment Agency have estimated a capital investment of £700,000 is required, together with yearly maintenance costs of £250,000. It has been suggested that the £700,000 could be found, but nobody will commit the maintenance costs. If this situation remains unchanged, it will result in **disaster**.

Northumberland Wildlife Trust is urging people to write to their local MP, and increase the pressure on the Government to find the money required. The Environment Agency will also be organising a public meeting for local people.

-ends-

Note to News Editors

Northumberland Wildlife Trust is the largest conservation body in the region. The Trust works to protect threatened wildlife in wild places in Northumberland and North Tyneside. Managing over 60 nature reserves in the country, the charity has over 5,000 members and a network of active local and special interest groups.

David Stewart, Chief Executive of Northumberland Wildlife Trust, will only be available for interview on Thursday 11 June at 4.30 pm. If you require further information, please contact Rachael Bradely, Marketing Officer on 0191 2846884.

Notes on Whittle Colliery

When Whittle Colliery was a working mine, more than 1 million gallons of minewater were pumped to the surface each day, and were treated before discharge into the rivers. Pumping stopped in March 1997 when the mine was abandoned after the owner, Stonegate Mining Ltd, went bankrupt. Under current legislation, there is no legal owner who is responsible for what is happening at the site. The regulatory bodies have no power until the pollution reaches the waterways and the damage is done.

Questions on passage D

The events in the newspaper reports you read (passages A–C) have already taken place.

Passage D concerns an event that has not yet taken place. However, the piece of writing is not science fiction such as *The Day of the Triffids*. It is yet another different style.

1. How do you know it is not science fiction?

2. Is it non-fiction? How do you know?

3. What is the point of the passage?

4. How has the passage been structured?

5. Which words show clearly how important the writer feels this matter is?

Poetry

Teachers' introduction

The selection of poetry that follows is obviously not exhaustive or prescribed. Teachers can use others poems with which they are familiar. There are a number of 'environmental' poems around, but many of them are 'verse' rather than 'poetry'. This selection is an attempt to expose pupils to quality poetry, and at the same time to look at how:

- poets handle a subject differently at different periods of history
- a topic can be handled differently through different styles of writing.

All of this leads very naturally to a critical evaluation of literature (CEL).

Note that it is no bad thing to insert a weaker poem into a series of quality poems for pupils to grasp the distinction. For obvious reasons copyright clearance has not been sought for inclusion of a 'bad' poem.

The selection is readily available in many anthologies and is largely familiar to teachers. This is deliberate. It has simply been collated here for the convenience of teachers.

Other poems suitable for use are:

- 'The Hare' by Sydney Tremayne
- 'On the Death of an Emperor Penguin in Regent's Park' by David Wright
- 'To See the Rabbit' by Alan Brownjohn
- 'The Hawk' by George Mackay Brown
- 'A Man in Assynt' by Norman MacCaig.

Pupils' introduction

For centuries, poets have written about the natural world around them in many different ways. Their varieties of attitude differ as widely as their styles of writing, and yet both the attitudes and the writing styles have in common their construction through the dominant ideas of their time. The romantic poets, for example, celebrated nature in a way that we now find quite strange. Wordsworth, in the main, saw the city as representative of sin and rural life as idyllic. At the time of writing, Britain was in the throes of the upheaval of the Industrial Revolution. Cities were growing, the agricultural life and the social infrastructure of the country were being altered for ever. The poetry reflected this.

Poetry is a term given to highly concentrated writing that rests broadly on rhythm and imagery. Many poets see their task as two-fold: to work to perfection with the form of the text they are writing, that is by polishing sound, rhythm, imagery, structure, perhaps rhyme; and to make observations on the world as they see it.

There follows a selection of poems that deal with the natural world in a variety of ways.

Each poem should lead to a deeper understanding of how poetry works to make meaning. Collectively and separately they provide insights into human patterns of behaviour.

Poem A

Hawk Roosting
Ted Hughes

I sit in the top of the wood, my eyes closed.
Inaction, no falsifying dream
Between my hooked head and hooked feet:
Or in sleep rehearse perfect kills and eat.

The convenience of the high trees!
The air's buoyancy and the sun's ray
Are of advantage to me;
And the earth's face upward for my inspection.

My feet are locked upon the rough bark.
It took the whole of Creation
To produce my foot, my each feather:
Now I hold Creation in my foot

Or fly up, and revolve it all slowly –
I kill where I please because it is all mine.
There is no sophistry in my body:
My manners are tearing off heads –

The allotment of death.
For the one path of my flight is direct
Through the bones of the living.
No arguments assert my right:

The sun is behind me.
Nothing has changed since I began.
My eye has permitted no change.
I am going to keep things like this.

By kind permission of Faber and Faber Ltd

Poem B

An Otter
Ted Hughes

I

Underwater eyes, an eel's
Oil of water body, neither fish nor beast is the otter:
  Four-legged yet water-gifted, to outfish fish;
    With webbed feet and long ruddering tail
    And a round head like an old tomcat.

    Brings the legend of himself
From before wars or burials, in spite of hounds and vermin-poles;
  Does not take root like the badger. Wanders, cries;
    Gallops along land he no longer belongs to;
    Re-enters the water by melting.

    Of neither water nor land. Seeking
Some world lost when first he dived, that he cannot come at since,
  Takes his changed body into the holes of lakes;
    As if blind, cleaves the stream's push till he licks
    The pebbles of the source; from sea

    To sea crosses in three nights
Like a king in hiding. Crying to the old shape of the starlit land,
  Over sunken farms where the bats go round,
    Without answer. Till light and birdsong come
    Walloping up roads with the milk wagon.

II

The hunt's lost him. Pads on mud,
Among sedges, nostrils a surface bead,
The otter remains, hours. The air,
Circling the globe, tainted and necessary,

Mingling tobacco-smoke, hounds and parsley,
Comes carefully to the sunk lungs.
So the self under the eye lies,
Attendant and withdrawn. The otter belongs

In double robbery and concealment –
From water that nourishes and drowns, and from land
That gave him his length and the mouth of the hound.
He keeps fat in the limpid integument

Reflections live on. The heart beats thick,
Big trout muscle out of the dead cold;
Blood is the belly of logic; he will lick
The fishbone bare. And can take stolen hold

On a bitch otter in a field full
Of nervous horses, but linger nowhere.
Yanked above hounds, reverts to nothing at all,
To this long pelt over the back of a chair.

By kind permission of Faber and Faber Ltd

Poem C

Hill Being Organ
Norman MacCaig

I once heard
Blunt Suilven throb tremolo and deep down
In an Atlantic gale. I was half-frightened.
Bach would have loved it.

It was as if
A tree were to dance in a Scotch, not Bali way,
Flinging about its field, almost saying Hooch
Like a Scot in a story.

There are other
Differences between me and Bach, but that is one.
He had the advantage, of course; he knew the language
The mountain was speaking.

One thing –
The quirky trebles sounded in the loch below –
I could understand them, agreeably ornamenting
That ferocious ground bass.

A good job, else
I would be frightened of Bach, except when he
Danced like a tree not moving – just imagine
Bach saying Hooch.

By kind permission of Hogarth Press

Poem D

To a Mountain Daisy

Robert Burns

On turning one down, with the plough, in April 1786

Wee, modest, crimson-tippèd flow'r,
Thou's met me in an evil hour;
For I maun crush amang the stoure
     Thy slender stem:
To spare thee now is past my pow'r,
      Thou bonie gem.

Alas! It's no thy neebor sweet,
The bonie Lark, companion meet!
Bending thee 'mang the dewy weet!
     Wi' spreckl'd breast,
When upward-springing, blythe, to greet
      The purpling East.

Cauld blew the bitter-biting North
Upon thy early, humble birth;
Yet chearfully thou glinted forth
     Amid the storm,
Scarce rear'd above the Parent-earth
      Thy tender form.

The flaunting flow'rs our Gardens yield,
High shelt'ring woods and wa's maun shield;
But thou, beneath the random bield
     O' clod or stane,
Adorns the histie stibble-field
      Unseen, alane.

There, in thy scanty mantle clad,
The snawie bosom sun-ward spread,
Thou lifts thy unassuming head
     In humble guise;
But now the share uptears thy bed,
      And low thy lies!

Such is the fate of artless Maid,
Sweet flow'ret of the rural shade!
By Love's simplicity betray'd,
     And guileless trust,
Till she, like thee, all soil'd, is laid
      Low i' the dust.

Such is the fate of simple Bard,
On life's rough ocean luckless starr'd!
Unskilful he to note the card
     Of prudent Lore,
Till billows rage, and gales blow hard,
      And whelm him o'er!

Such fate to suffering Worth is giv'n,
Who long with wants and woes has striv'n,
By human pride or cunning driv'n
     To Mis'ry's brink,
Till wrench'd of ev'ry stay but Heav'n,
      He, ruin'd, sink!

Ev'n thou who mourn'st the Daisy's fate,
That fate is thine – no distant date;
Stern Ruin's plough-share drives, elate,
     Full on thy bloom,
Till crush'd beneath the furrow's weight,
      Shall be thy doom!

Poem E

To a Mouse
Robert Burns

Wee, sleekit, cowrin', tim'rous beastie,
O, what a panic's in thy breastie!
Thou need na start awa sae hasty,
Wi' bickering brattle!
I wad be laith to rin an' chase thee,
Wi' murd'ring pattle!

I'm truly sorry man's dominion,
Has broken Nature's social union,
An' justifies that ill opinion,
Which makes thee startle
At me, thy poor, earth-born companion,
An' fellow-mortal!

I doubt na, whiles, but thou may thieve;
What then? poor beastie, thou maun live!
A daimen icker in a thrave
'S a sma' request;
I'll get blessin wi' the lave,
An' never miss't!

Thy wee bit housie, too, in ruin!
It's silly wa's the win's are strewin!
An' naething, now, to big a new ane,
O' foggage green!
An' bleak December's winds ensuin,
Baith snell an' keen!

Thou saw the fields laid bare an' waste,
An' weary winter comin fast,
An' cozie here, beneath the blast,
Thou thought to dwell –
Till crash! The cruel coulter past
Out thro' thy cell.

That wee bit heap o' leaves an' stibble,
Has cost thee monie a weary nibble!
Now thou's turn'd out, for a' thy trouble,
But house or hald,
To thole the winter's sleety dribble,
An' cranreuch cauld!

But Mousie, thou art no thy lane,
In proving foresight may be vain;
The best-laid schemes o' mice an' men
Gang aft agley,
An' lea'e us nought but grief an' pain,
For promis'd joy!

Still thou art blest, compar'd wi' me!
The present only toucheth thee:
But och! I backward cast my e'e,
On prospects drear!
An' forward, tho' I canna see,
I guess an' fear!

Poem F

The Starlings in George Square
Edwin Morgan

I

Sundown on the high stonefields!
The darkening roofscape stirs –
thick – alive with starlings
gathered singing in the square –
like a shower of arrows they cross
the flash of a western window,
they bead the wires with jet,
they nestle preening by the lamps
and shine, sidling by the lamps
and sing, shining, they stir
the homeward hurrying crowds.
A man looks up and points
smiling to his son beside him
wide-eyed at the clamour on those cliffs –
it sinks, shrills out in waves,
levels to a happy murmur,
scatters in swooping arcs,
a stab of confused sweetness
that pierces the boy like a story,
a story more than a song.
He will never forget that evening,
the silhouette of the roofs,
the starling by the lamps.

II

The City Chambers are hopping mad.
Councillors with rubber plugs in their ears!
Secretaries closing windows!
Window-cleaners want protection and danger money.
The Lord Provost can't hear herself think, man.
What's that?
Lord Provost, can't hear herself think.

At the General Post Office
the clerks write Three Pounds Starling in the savings-books.
Each telephone-booth is like an aviary.
I tried to send a parcel to County Kerry but –
The cables to Cairo got fankled, sir.
What's that?
I said the cables to Cairo got fankled.

And as for the City Information Bureau –
I'm sorry I can't quite chirrup did you twit –
No I wanted to twee but perhaps you can't cheep –

Would you try once again, that's better, I – sweet –
When's the last boat to Milngavie? Tweet?
What's that?
I said when's the last boat to Milngavie?

III

There is nothing for it now but scaffolding:
clamp it together, send for the bird-men,
Scarecrow Strip for the window-ledge landings,
Cameron's Repellent on the overhead wires.
Armour our pediments against eavesdroppers.
This is a human outpost. Save our statues.
Send back the jungle. And think of the joke:
as it says in the papers, It is very comical
to watch them alight on the plastic rollers
and take a tumble. So it doesn't kill them?
All right, so who's complaining? This isn't Peking
where they shoot the sparrows for hygiene and cash.
So we're all humanitarians, locked in our cliff-dwellings
encased in our repellent, guano-free and guilt-free.
The Lord Provost sings in her marble hacienda.
The Postmaster-General licks an audible stamp.
Sir Walter is vexed that his column's deserted.
I wonder if we really deserve starlings?
There is something to be said for these joyous messengers
that we repel in our indignant orderliness.
They lift up the eyes, they lighten the heart,
and some day we'll decipher that sweet frenzied whistling
as they wheel and settle along our hard roofs
and take those grey buttresses for home.
One thing we know they say, after their fashion.
They like the warm cliffs of man.

Edwin Morgan, *The Second Life*, 1968, reprinted in
Edwin Morgan: Collected Poems, Carcanet Press Limited

Drama

Teachers' notes

'Wormwood' by Catherine Czerkauska deals with Chernobyl. Within the play the nuclear arguments are debated prior to the disaster. The text progresses to the events following the accident and the effect on both people and the environment are explicit. The story is seen through the eyes of a survivor, and centres on the potential for disaster when nuclear energy and human fallibility are intertwined.

It would make an ideal text for S3/S4. Its 'message' is very clear. It is skilfully written, with strong character development and a structure comprehensible to Standard Grade pupils.

There are detailed notes on this text in *Working with Scottish Plays* support notes, published by Learning and Teaching Scotland (formerly Scottish CCC). This is available in Scottish secondary schools.

'Whale' by David Holman deals with a stranded whale, and would be more suited to General pupils. Foundation pupils would find this stretching, but not impossible.

Media studies

Teachers' introduction

Reading the media can be done either through print or through the moving image.

Many of the texts in other sections of this publication are newspaper articles, so the structure of a news story, and the language in which it is written, have already been looked at. What follows below is a study of the moving image. This can be submitted for critical evaluation of literature (CEL).

Before embarking on this study, pupils should already be familiar with the concepts of 'representation' and 'narrative', either from work already done in S1 and S2, or from work done in preparation for studying the film.

The following support notes cover all necessary aspects for the Media CEL for Standard Grade English. They are based on the film *Free Willie*.

Free Willie

Pupils should watch this film straight through and then carry out the work that follows. The notes here are not intended to teach teachers how to teach media studies. They are written to illustrate what is necessary for studying a full-length film with a Standard Grade class in order to lead to a CEL in media.

Teachers can decide whether or not to teach didactically or through (assessable) discussion.

Narrative
There are two narratives operating:
• the fortunes of the whale
• the fortunes of the child.

They are brought together through the interaction of the child and the whale. The whale is a civilising force on the child, and the child in return frees, and loses, the whale thereby rendering the ending more poignant than many happy-ever-after-ending adult films. In the process the child becomes amenable to the adults, who in turn are influenced by the needs of the whale. Thus the internal child of the adult is satisfied by the resolution. Only the bad adults lose out. The film has a classic structure.

The key scenes that benefit from close examination are:
• the opening scene
• when Jesse meets his foster parents

- when Jesse meets Willie
- when Willie refuses to perform
- the rescue sequences.

They need to be looked at through:
- *mis en scène*
- representation
- language of film.

Mis en scène/Montage

The film opens with a very attractive scene. The lighting and the colours sparkle. The whales are graceful and playful. When the boat comes along, there is both aural and visual montage to construct the 'baddies'. The words 'Free Willie' make a circle like the rope of the net in which he is caught. This then cuts to a circular plaza – an example of montage to connect visually the whale and the child.

When Jesse meets the Greenwoods, their house is very comfortable. The room he is given is beautifully decorated, yet he rejects this. Thus Jesse's personal quest is set up as outside the materialistic strand of the American dream. This is displayed by the slow pan shot of the room, which distances Jesse from it. It is shot at his level but he is apart. He does not simply want money: he wants his mother. In contrast, when he meets the whale the scene is shot in close-up to emphasise the intimacy of the child and the whale. There is water, child and whale, which contrasts with all the trappings of the house he has rejected.

It is after the whale fails to perform that Jesse faces up to the truth about his mother. He says to Willie, 'Have a good life', and walks away. The whale cries. Thus the two stories are pulled together in Jesse leaving Willie 'on the doorstep'. This is followed by the whale's family returning and Jesse's need for the Greenwoods.

The rescue scenes are shot largely in the dark, but when Willie finally escapes, the colours and the lighting are vivid as at the beginning. Thus the route is set up through the interaction of adult and child to help the whale escape, and then for the child to accept the family and the lifestyle represented by the house. The car wash sequence has been edited to let us see how the car wash gives Jesse an idea. The music changes as the baddies drive past and this is followed by a close-up of Jesse reassuring Willie. However a contrasting montage in sound and plot is then inserted: the baddies turn back. Another close-up indicates IDEA, and this is accompanied by the theme music, which indicates the idea will be successful. The sequence then alternates between success and failure until Willie escapes. This is mirrored by Jesse running along the breakwater as the whale leaps to freedom. The last scene is washed in daylight, with the dawn sun rising over the mountains, and ricochets between reaction shots, until Jesse cuddles up to the Greenwoods and says, 'Can I go home?', while Willie plays in the water in a slow motion shot.

Representation

Initially although the children are behaving in a way that would be considered unacceptable, they are shot in close-up, emphasising their point of view. Thus the audience is led to sympathise with them. The adults are constructed as either do-gooders or wicked. The owner of the whale is prepared to let it die for the insurance money. Throughout the film he is never seen as happy, or out of a business suit. The goodness in Jesse is set in opposition to this man's greed and Jesse rescues the whale from the wickedness of money-grabbing adults. This allows the friendly adults to key into their 'realness' and so they help him. Thus, they are constructed more as good children than bad adults.

The representation is explicit. Children are basically decent, and the child in all of us needs to be realised to create an environmentally better world. Only when that happens can Jesse live with the trappings of the adult world. Children are caring. Children can also be lonely, sad and angry with good reason. (Jesse has been abandoned by an uncaring adult.)

It is also worth noting that Jesse goes along with the performing tricks to raise money to get Willie a better pool to give him more space. He is involved in the exploitation of Willie for the whale, not for the adults.

Jesse hates when the Greenwoods fight. Conflict clearly has appalling memories for him. The camera technique here of the shot closing in on him is similar to a scene in *Close Encounters of the Third Kind* where the child hears his parents fighting as he stands beside a closing door.

Almost immediately after this scene, Jesse tells his mates that his situation 'could be worse'. He is accepting being with the Greenwoods and is then able to work more closely with Willie, thus moving to the resolution of the film.

The whale is represented as good. It means no evil and does no harm. It has feelings. (It is interesting that the story is about a whale, not a shark. Whales are perceived as more friendly. *Jaws* has not been kind to the representation of sharks.)

Both Randolph and the trainer have links with native American extraction. They are closer to the whale through their culture and their stories, and so ultimately help the whale to escape using an old chant. White capitalism is isolated as evil.

Willie is lost and lonely as is the little boy. Thus it touches us all through the representation of fear of being lost, and of separation from our families. It is worth exploring the similarity between *Free Willie* and *ET*. A child in a less than happy situation, yet surrounded by the trappings of American middle-class comfort, makes contact with a non-human and rescues it, but in the process loses it, to make it possible to finally regain family. Adults are the enemy, since they have lost touch with their sense of wonder in their reckless pursuit of, in *ET*, science and, in *Free Willie*, money. Other similarities are:

- both 'aliens' learned things (Willie how to do tricks/ET how to talk)
- Jesse on the bike with fish in the basket/Elliott on the bike with ET in the basket
- the opening scenes with ET left behind/Willie left behind
- both families return for their lost child/ET's family return
  – whales come back (unlike Jesse's mother, who has abandoned him)
- both involve young boys (would the films have been so popular if girls had been the leading characters?)
- happy endings
- middle-class suburbs.

The family is reinforced because not only do the children return to the family – ET and Willie do also.

Language of film

There is extensive use of close-ups in the scenes between the child and the whale. This suggests intimacy in contrast with longer shots when Jesse is with the adults. The first time Jesse sees the whale a gentle shot has been used. There is no sense of fear. It is a slow shot across the screen. When Jesse is feeding Willie an eye-level camera shot is used to show Jesse becoming braver. As Jesse touches Willie, the camera closes in on the hand to emphasise his daring. The music tells us that the whale will not bite him. This is followed by a close-up of Jesse's face to show intensity. Another example would be that the first time he uses the mouth organ it is in close up.

There is also extensive use of montage to set up the different representations, and to drive the narrative – especially in the rescue scenes.

The lighting is significant. The brightness disappears as the story becomes darker in order to re-emerge at the end. The slow-motion shots in the light at the end are very pretty and reflect the story at that point.

The music tells the story side by side with the words. There are many examples of sound bridges to indicate what is about to happen. This helps to build up the narrative, and create excitement for the audience. The scene when Jesse falls in the water makes extensive use of music. It begins with no sound, and then there is one long blast as Jesse slips into the water. The music builds up as Willie swims towards Jesse. The whale touches him, and we do not know what will happen, but the music becomes gentle as Willie lays Jesse on the side of the pool. (The scene is also shot in blue to add to the danger element, until the moonlight falls across the screen.) It is also placed immediately after the conversation about killer whales – further use of montage. The interaction of music, *mis en scène* and plot are also clear in the scene when Willie refuses to perform. The music is jolly, and then the banging of the children on the tank is accompanied by a close-up of Willie's eye. The noise and the bars indicate how Willie is trapped. There is no music. The banging is used to make the scene more uncomfortable. The music becomes scary and the accompanying shot is of Willie's teeth. As Jesse panics, the music reinforces this.

All of this makes explicit the ideology of the movie, which is that whales are decent creatures and should not be exploited by humans, who are essentially driven by greed. Hope for the future lives in children. They will create a better world. The film is followed by a Save the Whale advertisement!

Follow-up work to *Free Willie* could also include a general discussion on the difference between the 'whales' message of *Free Willie* and the 'sharks' message of *Jaws*.

Practical exercise

Many people think that environmental concerns are only for the inhabitants of rural areas. Clearly this is not the case. City dwellers rely on the air they breathe, and the farm-produced food they eat, every bit as much as do rural dwellers.

Using the interaction of words and images, in groups, design an advert whose target market lives in cities. The purpose of the advert is to make city dwellers aware of their role in biodiversity.

The advert may be for newspapers, radio, TV, cinema or billboards.

The target age group has to be decided, as that will affect language and images. The advert must make people aware of their responsibility for their own behaviour, on a day-to-day basis rather than limiting their involvement to fund-raising campaigns.

TALK (DISCUSSION)

Teachers' introduction

As this is discussion work, the groups need to be prepared for discussion techniques in the way the teacher would normally use.

This unit of work does not teach discussion skills. Rather it makes available texts and topics that will allow for class discussion, and suggests questions/activities to prompt discussion.

The texts have not been labelled 'Foundation', 'General' or 'Credit'. To do so would be to divide on reading levels, and that is not in the spirit of discussion work. To allow weaker pupils the opportunity to access some of the difficult pieces of text, they could in pairs break down the texts paragraph by paragraph. This of course would allow for practising reading and précis skills, and would be a preliminary lesson on its own. It would make it possible for pupils to access difficult passages in order to handle the concepts in discussion. The source material is of varied reading levels to allow teachers the opportunity of using it across all levels. It has to be said, however, that topics 4, 5 and 6 require more advanced reading skills.

Pupils' introduction

In this section you will study a range of articles and try to develop a policy that makes it possible for conservationists, farmers and others whose livelihood depends on the land, city dwellers – indeed, all of us – to work together to turn the spiral of human destruction in the opposite direction.

'Biodiversity' is a word made from 'biological' and 'diversity'. It means 'all living things', their interdependency and interlinking. In the past the word 'nature' might have been used to mean something similar.

All around us we hear much about saving dolphins or saving whales. Biodiversity looks at the planet in a different way. It is not a single-issue word, but rather it is used to cover the 'variety of life forms, the ecological roles they perform and the genetic diversity they contain'.

Human beings are damaging this planet we live on. Many people are now very concerned about this, and wish to move humans away from our present course of destruction. It is worth looking back to previous centuries. The North American peoples believed that the Earth supported all life, from insects to humans, by providing food for all living beings. They respected the Earth for its function, and had no concept of owning it. This simple fact was the root cause of the conflict between the native Americans, and the land-acquiring white people in the wagon trains that rolled across the prairie last century.

Step into this century and the conflict remains the same. Some individuals and companies own vast lands, and this affects the lives of people and animals living on them.

Many farmers are in conflict with conservationists.

Topics

Topic 1

Many city dwellers shrug their shoulders over biodiversity. How can they be made aware that their lives are part of 'nature', and that what happens in the countryside affects them too?

Work in groups.

1.   Make up a list of what in the city you perceive as part of nature, for example, trees in the parks.

2.   Think beyond this to what comes into the city from outside that is part of nature, for example, the water supply. Make up a list of everything you can think of that goes into the city from outside.

3.   Now make a third list of what goes from the city to the countryside.

4.   Look at your lists and discuss what city dwellers can do to protect the countryside and the city.

Topic 2

What would you give up to make the world a pleasant place for your children?

Work in groups.

1.   Discuss examples of how we are affecting the planet we live on.

Topic 3

Do you think it would be better to address concerns about the planet as single issues or under the heading of biodiversity? Look at both sides of the argument and come to a conclusion.

Work in groups.

1.   Make a list of the concerns people express about the planet. Some people are concerned about whales, others about dolphins. What other environmental issues are you aware of?

2.   Discuss whether or not these issues would be better tackled under the term 'biodiversity' than as single-issue concerns.

Topic 4

For this topic there are two items to read, 'Biodiversity: In a Nutshell' and 'Prime Time for Foes of the Earth', which presents the anti-environmentalist argument.

Find the main points in each argument, and discuss which point of view you think is right.

Work in groups.

1.   Identify the main arguments presented in 'Biodiversity: In a Nutshell' by reading the article carefully.

2.   Identify the main arguments in 'Prime Time for Foes of the Earth' by reading the article carefully.

3.   List the two sets of arguments.

4.   Discuss the arguments and come to a conclusion about how society should move forward, in relation to environmental concerns.

Topic 4 extract 1

BIODIVERSITY: IN A NUTSHELL

'Biodiversity, the planet's most valuable resource, is on loan to us from our children.'

Biodiversity is a recently-made-up word which is closely associated with major international initiatives to protect the world's natural heritage. This information sheet looks at biodiversity as 'a big new idea', explains why it is important, and suggests what we, as individuals, can do to help. The word biodiversity is short for 'biological diversity', and can be summarised as 'the total variety of all living things'. A simple definition states that biodiversity includes:

… the variety of life forms, the ecological roles they perform, and the genetic diversity they contain.

OUR LIVING BANK BALANCE

Although we may not readily appreciate it, biodiversity provides us with many of the things that sustain our lives. It is essential for our wellbeing that we protect biodiversity – the variations in species, their lives and their habitats – biodiversity is necessary for our quality of life and our standard of living.

Biodiversity is an essential part of our *cultural heritage*.

Plants and animals are part of our traditions and culture. The thistle is our national emblem, proudly emblazoned on the jerseys of rugby players. The 'bonnie purple heather' and the aptly-named Scots Pine are special parts of Scotland's countryside, of which we are rightly proud. Scotland's wild landscapes, plants and animals are also key assets for our tourist industry. People come from far afield to admire the colours and patterns of the Scottish countryside – features which are themselves produced by biodiversity – or to see rare species like red squirrels, golden eagles and ospreys, or the teeming seabird cliffs of our coasts.

Biodiversity is a hidden treasure that enriches all our lives. Few of us will ever see a giant panda, a pine marten or a whale in the wild, but most of us would like to know that we might have a chance to see them one day. And biodiversity is not just about rarities. The skylark, the primrose, and the garden spider are equally important parts of Scotland's biodiversity.

Biodiversity is essential because of its *economic importance*.

All farm crops and animals are descendants of wild organisms, and they are also a component of biodiversity. Some old crop varieties have more taste or disease resistance,

and they may be better suited to future changes in the climate. Fruit crops rely on the many insects that pollinate their flowers. We also take food from the wild, like venison or salmon. Fisherman, with their nets and rods, are simply harvesting the natural biodiversity of the oceans or rivers.

Biodiversity is essential as a provider of *natural services*.

The natural world also provides many services, which we may not always readily recognise. Peat bogs, for example, have an important role in purifying water and in locking up carbon dioxide, one of the gases produced from the burning of fossil fuels that are causing 'global warming'. The tiny plants that float in the top few metres of the sea also absorb huge amounts of this carbon dioxide, as long as the sea remains healthy.

Every living thing has a place in what we call the 'balance of nature', and upsetting that balance can have untold effects, from which, more often than not, we are the losers.

Biodiversity is essential as a source of *natural products*.

Although we are able to produce more and more drugs synthetically, we still rely on plants for many of our medicines. Medicines for heart disease, for example, are still produced today from wild foxgloves. Wild plants are constantly being screened in search

Topic 4 extract 1 (continued)

of cures for cancer, AIDS and other diseases. We can never tell which species might prove useful: chemicals extracted from jellyfish, for example, are now being used by medical researchers studying the development of cancers.

Biodiversity is an essential part of *sustainable development*.

Biodiversity is a measure of sustainable development – growth today that does not deprive the quality of life of future generations. Sustainable development is regarded as a major target for industry and the planning system, and measuring biodiversity is the only way to be sure that this target is being achieved.

> *Biodiversity is part of our daily lives and livelihoods, and constitutes the resources upon which families, communities, nations and future generations depend.*

UNDER THREAT

Yet, despite its importance, biodiversity is under threat all around us. Through inappropriate forms of development and too intensive agriculture, we are damaging our wild countryside and reducing the variety of life it can support. Also pollution from industry and the unwise use of energy restricts the capacity of the soil and water to support life, and overfishing is reducing the richness of the seas and rivers.

SHARING THE BENEFITS

The word 'biodiversity' came from the Earth Summit held in Rio de Janeiro in 1992, where 159 countries (including Britain) recognised the value of biodiversity to human life, and signed what was to become known as the Biodiversity Convention. This pledges the UK to conserve biodiversity, to use its components in a way that will ensure they continue to be available for future generations and share the benefits of biodiversity fairly and equitably between all nations and people.

Britain has since taken the lead internationally in turning these ideas into plans for action. The Government has commissioned a detailed programme of recommendations, known as the 'UK Biodiversity Action Plan', to ensure that national policies help to protect our biodiversity assets.

BIODIVERSITY IN SCOTLAND

In Scotland, the Scottish Biodiversity Group was set up by the Secretary of State to take forward Biodiversity in Scotland. The Group includes representatives from The Scottish Office, government environment agencies, local authorities, conservation groups, universities and research institutes, and fishing, farming, crofting and landowning interests. It is therefore a unique, broadly-based partnership of those who work in, depend on and care for Scotland's countryside.

The Scottish Group is overseeing the production and implementation of action plans for plants and animals which are either predominantly or wholly found in Scotland (such as corncrakes, red squirrels and chequered skipper butterflies), and habitat action plans for Scotland's most special wild places, including pine forests, blanket bogs and the machair of the Western Isles. The Government is seeking 'champions' from industry and commerce to assist with the work that must be done. The Scottish Group is also supporting the production of Local Biodiversity Action Plans, now being prepared by local authorities throughout Scotland. As the title suggests, these reflect the biodiversity of local areas and require the active involvement of local communities.

BIODIVERSITY AND YOU!

Everyone has a role – and a responsibility to conserve biodiversity. Using energy wisely, using our cars less and public transport more, making more use of environmentally-friendly and recycled products, eating more organic food, and recycling more of our rubbish, are all positive ways to help. Creating a wild corner in our gardens, with nectar-rich flowers to attract butterflies and plentiful seeds and fruits for the birds, can provide a 'haven of biodiversity'. Even a suitably-planted window-box can help bring life to a city street. You could also make sure your local council is producing a Local Biodiversity Action Plan, offer your own ideas to help develop this plan, and help your local community groups to involve others in this all-important task.

Scottish Biodiversity Group

Topic 4 extract 2

Prime time for foes of the Earth

UK: US-style anti-environmentalists to compare Greens with Nazis.

Nightmare scenario or scaremongering?
It depends on how you ignore the facts.

The backlash against environmentalism shifts up a gear in the UK later this month with the decision by Channel 4 to put out a peak-time series which attacks environmentalism for its 'anti-human' tendencies, compares it to Fascism and draws parallels between the beliefs of environmentalists and those of the Nazis.

Against Nature will consist of three one-hour programmes. It is avowedly propagandist and will probably constitute the most exhaustive airing anti-green views have received in the British media. Leading Greens such as Jonathon Porritt describe much of its content as idiotic and caution against it being taken too seriously. Others see it as part of the growing challenge by corporate interests to environmental 'orthodoxy' – and the attempt to export anti-green lobbying tactics from the US to Europe.

In the US, most observers believe that the anti-environmental lobby, though past its heyday of the early nineties, remains a potent force. This autumn, business and land-owning interests are pushing for changes which could seriously undermine legislation on habitat protection, endangered species and water cleanliness. Proposals before Congress seek to extend compensation payable to land-owners so that virtually any environmental legislation could be prohibitively expensive. Property owners, for instance, could claim compensation if laws forbade them from polluting waterways on their land or interfering with protected habitats.

The anti-green lobby derives much of its inspiration from Wise Use, the coalition set up in the US in 1988 with the aim of eradicating environmentalism. Dan Barry, of the Washington-based Environmental Working Group, which monitors anti-environmental activity, says the last Congress failed 'miserably' to push through its pro-business agenda and that, of 25 aims set by Wise Use at its launch, only one has been achieved – the introduction of federal subsidies for off-road-vehicle recreation on public land. But land-owning interests recently won the battle to keep tax concessions for 'private' logging or mining roads built on publicly owned land, and according to Sharon Buccino, a senior lawyer with the Natural Resources Defence Council, the new proposals on compensation constitute a 'real threat to the environment'.

Barry argues that the identification of Wise Use with extreme right-wing views and with big business has put off many American voters. 'They are still trying to play a good game in the media, but they don't have a constituency and they're not attracting new members.' But he concedes that, with large amounts of money at their disposal and powerful allies in Congress –

Topic 4 extract 2 (continued)

including the delegation from Alaska, currently at the centre of an oil-and-logging-v-wildlife conflict – 'they're not going to go away .... It's become a war of attrition.'

Martin Durkin, the producer of the new Channel 4 series, says he sympathises with Wise Uses's critique but the series is made from a left-wing perspective. It draws parallels with the 'blood and soil' beliefs of the Nazis – including their forest-worship and alleged vegetarianism – casts doubt on global warming and overpopulation and accuses the green movement of being against technology and progress. Last year, Durkin made a film for Channel 4 which defended scientific 'freedom', including experiments on animals. '[Channel 4] decided it had hit a raw nerve and thought something more broadly on the environmental movement could by very controversial. But it's not being outrageous for its own sake. We are firmly behind the argument.' Durkin says the series is 'in the form of a balanced film, but it's very polemical, even propagandist'. His own view is that environmentalism is 'insidious garbage'.

Among those interviewed are Tony Juniper, campaigns director of Friends of the Earth. He believes corporate and right-wing media interests have recently stepped up lobbying in advance of this December's summit on climate change in Kyoto but calls these 'desperation tactics'. Porritt says the views of a 'wacky' minority should not be given undue weight, 'but, equally, it's important not to be complacent, as they were initially in the US. You need to refute such idiotic assertions as vigorously as possible.'

David Nicholson-Lord, 'Prime Time for Foes of the Earth', *BBC Wildlife*, November 1997

Topic 5

The article entitled 'Rights and wrongs' looks at the rights of indigenous people and gives arguments for and against the issue. Find the main points in the arguments and discuss whether or not you agree with them.

Work in groups.

1.   Identify the points of the passage to focus the purpose of the discussion.

2.   Discuss the arguments you have been presented with and consider whether you agree with them.

3.   What do you think should be the way forward?

Topic 5 extract

Rights and Wrongs

Should indigenous peoples have different 'rights' to hunt wildlife, including endangered species, and to trade in wildlife products? *David Lavigne* reports.

Participants at October's meeting of the International Whaling Commission in Monaco have considered a controversial application by Makah Indians from Washington State to obtain a permit to kill five grey whales. Much of the debate will have centred on the 'rights' of indigenous peoples to conduct 'traditional' subsistence and ceremonial whaling.

The issue of indigenous peoples' rights to hunt wildlife is fraught with controversy. Individuals and organisations with an interest in wildlife all have their own views. In other words, the answer to the question will depend on who is providing the answer.

Controversy notwithstanding, a number of jurisdictions have spoken quite decisively, at least on part of the question. Consistently, they have answered – yes, indigenous peoples should indeed have different legal rights than non-natives to hunt wildlife, including endangered species, at least for subsistence purposes. Such rights are entrenched, for example, in the US Marine Mammal Protection Act of 1972, in the Canadian Constitution Act of 1982 and the national legislation of other countries, including Australia and New Zealand. The special status of indigenous peoples to hunt certain wildlife is also recognised in various international agreements, such as in Agenda 21 (which arose out of the 1992 Earth Summit in Rio).

The issue remains complicated, however, on at least two fronts. First, many native peoples hold the view that they have the inherent right to hunt wildlife and dispute the authority of modern society to impose any restrictions on their activities. In Canada, for example, native peoples have long been fighting for the right of self-determination as 'First Nations'. Many regard any attempts to legislate their activities as 'cultural imperialism'.

At the other end of that particular spectrum is the view recently expressed by Canadian conservative Link Byfield that, to treat native people differently – such as by giving them special rights – is patronising. 'Special status,' writes Byfield, 'means lower status.'

Topic 5 extract (continued)

The second and major problem is that most hunting concessions granted to native peoples are usually restricted to 'traditional subsistence hunting'. Most people, and most conservationists, environmentalists and animal-welfare organisations, support the rights of indigenous people to exploit wildlife for use in their communities for food, clothing and shelter. Trade within and amongst indigenous communities is also generally accepted as part of traditional use. Disagreements surface, however, when indigenous peoples incorporate modern technologies – leghold traps, rifles with telescopic sights, snow-machines and powerful outboard motors – into 'traditional hunts', and when they want to sell wildlife products in the international marketplace.

Modern technologies and international commercial trade, it is often argued, are not part of a traditional lifestyle. Moreover, there are very big differences between hunting for subsistence (as defined above) and for the marketplace. The former usually means that hunters take only what they need, which is usually far less than what might be sustainably removed from a wildlife population. The latter, driven by the desire to maximise earnings, means that hunters will attempt to take many more animals than required in their communities.

A number of native groups and anthropologists maintain that it is inappropriate to define subsistence hunting so narrowly. They argue that indigenous cultures must be allowed to evolve and that, in the process, traditions change. And, as traditions change, so too does the definition of 'subsistence hunting'. At the 1985 CITES conference, the Canadian government, for example, redefined subsistence hunting to include any form of activity that turns an animal into 'hard cash'. The argument is that indigenous

people must be allowed to sell the products of their hunts on international markets to earn money to buy food, clothing, and other necessities of life for their families. From this perspective, commercial hunting is simply a component of subsistence hunting.

While Western society seems increasingly sympathetic to the attempts of indigenous peoples to sustain their cultures, it has yet to embrace wholeheartedly the view that market hunting for international trade is part of a traditional lifestyle. Recognising this, some native groups who wish to resurrect old traditions – such as the Makah – try to minimise opposition to their plans by stating that the products will be distributed and used locally 'in accordance with … traditional practice' and that 'none of the meat will be sold'.

But some native groups clearly want to open up markets to wildlife products. The Inuit Circumpolar Conference notes that Agenda 21 and the Universal Declaration on Rights of Indigenous People 'reaffirm indigenous peoples' rights and the need for humankind to develop industries based on the principle of sustainable utilisation.' And, to further that objective, such native groups have in recent years formed alliances with non-native groups that promote the commercial exploitation and international trade of wildlife products: the fur trade, commercial whalers and sealers, and other members of the so-called 'Wise Use Movement'.

By doing so, indigenous groups gain allies in their quest to open up hunting and trade in wildlife products. In the process, however, they remind us that the fate of exploited wildlife populations is determined, not by the ethnicity of the hunters, but by the methods and purposes for which they are hunted. And, it is problematic, if not impossible, in an era of economic globalisation and free trade, for any jurisdiction to grant different trading rights to indigenous peoples than those granted to non-native hunters.

Concern has also been expressed that, by joining such coalitions, indigenous peoples are allowing themselves to be 'used' by non-native exploiters of wildlife. The latter, the reasoning goes, are merely trying to regain support for their own endeavours by associating themselves with indigenous groups whose hunts are generally more tolerated in Western society.

Topic 5 extract (continued)

Proponents of this view cite evidence such as a 1985 document produced by the Canadian department of external affairs in which 'preservation of native cultures' was identified as an 'emotional theme' that could be used to counteract the activities of the anti-fur movement. The fur trade's stated strategy was designed – it is argued – to exploit society's concerns for indigenous peoples to prop up an industry under threat because of changing attitudes in Western society about the use of traps and the wearing of fur.

Why else, it has been asked, would the fur industry and certain governments suddenly become concerned about the fate of native people, after centuries of exploitation and neglect? And, why else would the World Council of Whalers – an international organisation with representatives from 10 countries (including Norway and Japan) – open an office, as it recently did, on Indian lands in British Columbia, where there has been no commercial whaling for decades?

Some indigenous groups, however, counter with charges that it is Western animal-rights groups which 'use' sympathetic indigenous people to further their very different agenda.

Regardless, history has taught us that regulated hunting for personal use – whether by native peoples for what used to be called subsistence or by non-native 'sport' hunters – can be a sustainable activity, as the past 70 years of North American wildlife management have demonstrated. In contrast, commercial hunting for the marketplace has frequently been linked to population declines and endangerment. Today, we clearly have the technology to overexploit many animal species in our pursuit of economic gain, as the present state of world fisheries perhaps most clearly attests.

The exponentially increasing human population also means, in many cases, that demand for certain wildlife products is growing faster than their populations can support, especially given that the humans are rapidly taking over and destroying wildlife habitats.

Nonetheless, some will continue to argue that, yes, we should grant special rights to indigenous peoples (and to certain non-native hunters) to gain benefits from increased commercial consumptive use and trade of wildlife products. Others will maintain that such a decision will almost certainly place exploited wildlife populations at risk. One thing is certain – if society decides to grant special rights regardless, and the sceptics, are correct, both wildlife populations and indigenous cultures are likely to become increasingly endangered.

David Lavigne, 'Rights and Wrongs', *BBC Wildlife*, November 1997

Topic 5 extract (continued)

FOR

- For Inuit, and many other indigenous peoples, hunting is an economic necessity.
- We respect animals and regulate our hunting to ensure that it is sustainable.
- Without cash from animal products, many Inuit cannot afford to hunt or go out on the land.
- We are the first line of defence for the Arctic, which is threatened by Western corporations and governments.

A similar debate resonates in the Arctic, where Inuit (Eskimos) in Greenland, Canada, Alaska and Russia are fighting to protect their way of life from the advocacy of animal-rights and

Aqqaluk Lynge
President of the Inuit Circumpolar Conference

radical environmental organisations. We also hunt, fish and trap, but to us, as to many other indigenous peoples around the world, hunting is not a 'sport' – it is an economic necessity, for what we hunt, particularly whales, seals, caribou and various species of birds, we eat. We are also able to sell skins and furs for badly needed cash.

When hunting, Inuit travel hundreds of miles through terrain many would consider barren, even treacherous. But when travelling, we observe the environment and pass this knowledge on to our sons and daughters so they can acquire hunting skills and understand what it means to be Inuit.

We respect animals, for without them we would not exist, and regulate our hunting so there will always be sufficient animals to go round. Sustainable development is a concept that perhaps many in the UK have only recently considered. Inuit, on the other hand, have been living this concept for hundreds of years.

We observe directly the environment's rhythms and cycles. Inuit don't need government inspectors or the television to tell them what's going on; often it is the other way round. Because of this, Inuit are the first line of defence for the Arctic environment.

This is important, as the region is increasingly coveted by Western corporations and governments for its oil, gas and mineral resources, or as a shipping route connecting Japan with Europe and the US.
Our ability to hunt and look after the environment on which we depend is threatened by the activities of Western animal rights organisations. These well-funded and media-savvy organisations, representing mostly urban residents with little or no direct experience of 'wilderness', have persuaded governments and the EU to place restrictions on our animal products. It is now very difficult for us to sell seal skins, furs and other animal products in your markets. Indeed, the markets themselves have shrunk as consumers fear to be seen wearing furs and skins.

Inuit are not a law unto themselves, for our economy has been interlinked with the West's for many years. In short, we need to sell animal products to Europeans and North Americans to earn cash to buy rifles, snowmobiles, gasoline and other equipment needed if we are to hunt. Without cash from animal products, many Inuit cannot afford to hunt or go out on the land. The West's actions have taken a tremendous toll on Inuit. For example, the collapse of the seal market in the early 1980s caused huge increases in suicides and other social problems in our communities.

Inuit are resilient and adaptable. Without these qualities, we could not survive in the unforgiving Arctic climate. But we find it difficult to adapt to changes in trade and markets. Without the Inuit hunting and travelling the Arctic, following the steps of their ancestors, who will stand up for and protect this vast region? The animal rights lobby?

Topic 5 extract (continued)

AGAINST

- We have the right to whale only when it preserves an unbroken subsistence-hunting tradition.
- Whale hunters should respect the spirit of the whales and their tribe's traditions.
- We can make more than enough money by encouraging tourists to come to see whales.
- My tribe has become the pawn of those who want to resume commercial whaling operations.

Alberta 'Binki' Thompson
Makah elder

The Makah were once hunters of whales. That was more than 70 years ago, when killing whales was necessary for survival. People also had to walk more than 90 miles to collect berries. Today, we go to the grocery store.

There are some in my tribe who wish to see a return to whaling, and are appealing to the International Whaling Commission (IWC) to allow my tribe to hunt grey whales. There is no similar desire by these same people to go long-distance berry picking.

The advocates for whaling talk about reviving traditions and about saving our children from drugs, alcohol and violence. But how can we discourage violence by firing .50 calibre bullets into whales?

There is much talk of killing, yet no talk of respecting traditions, the spirit of the whales, the honour of our elders or being prepared for the sacrifices, the cleansing ceremonies, the prayers and the rituals that were woven into the fabric of our whaling societies.

Out Tribal Council wants to go whaling next spring. But, as yet, there have been no traditional preparations – they have not built a proper canoe or designed traditional tools, and they would appear to have little interest in doing so.

All that remains is the desire to kill – but for money, not subsistence, as we do not need whale meat to survive. Whereas we once hunted for the Makah, some now want to kill whales for the Japanese. We have become the pawns of countries such as Norway and Japan, who are using us in their global campaign to resume commercial whaling. Our culture will be a mask behind which these countries will profit.

Two years ago, when a whale was drowned in one of our nets, we did not know what to do with it or how to cut it up. In the end, most of the whale was carted to a rubbish dump. If we could not eat one whale then, how can we be expected to eat five or nine now?

The whale has come to live in peace among us. They attract tourists from all over the world. Such visitors, who could bring much-needed money into our communities, will not come when the whales have been frightened away.

The IWC defines aboriginal whaling as legitimate if it provides needed nourishment and preserves an 'unbroken' hunting tradition. Whaling is still an essential activity among some communities where wildlife is the only exploitable resource, and these people should be allowed to continue to hunt. But the Makah situation is clear – we do not need whale meat for nourishment, and our hunting tradition was broken 70 years ago. To start whaling again without re-establishing the spiritual aspect of these traditions is to dishonour our ancestors.

It is absurd that the Makah have hired a non-native ballistics expert to teach them how to kill a whale. He will not be able to teach them how to respect the whale and honour our traditions. Again, the emphasis is on killing and not our cultural heritage.

We must not let ourselves become the mercenary killers of whales for Japanese food markets. As an elder, I have an obligation to protect the dignity of our traditions and a responsibility to represent the concerns of our children.

For this reason, I attended the IWC meeting in Scotland in 1996 and will be attending this year's meeting in Monaco. And it is for this reason that I will continue to fight my tribe's proposal to hunt whales.

David Lavigne, 'Rights and Wrongs', *BBC Wildlife*, November 1997

Topic 6

The accompanying articles could be used as the focus for discussing the following questions.

Work in groups.

1. Do people feel the same concerns about spiders as they do for whales?

    If not, why not?

    Should they?

2. What form of protection can be provided for spiders on Arthur's Seat, which is surrounded by a main road and is a favourite place for Sunday walks?

    Would this protection make spiders more vulnerable, as it might attract people to look?

3. Two species of spider have only recently been rediscovered. Where does this fact fit in the biodiversity debate?

4. Do people feel differently about butterflies and ants?

    If so, why?

    Should they?

Topic 6 extract 1

Find of the century as jumping spider lands on Arthur's Seat

Andrew Walker

The world of arachnology has a keen-eyed postman to thank for two discoveries that are forcing experts to rewrite their records.

Stuart Maxwell has found two species of jumping spiders – they launch themselves at their prey – close to Edinburgh city centre.

One of the spiders, known as *Aelurillus v-insignatus*, was previously sighted in Fife 100 years ago by William Evans, an eminent naturalist, but has not been recorded since. The other – *Sitticus pubescens* – was last sighted more than 50 years ago on Skye.

The discovery of *Aelurillus v-insignatus* was made by Mr Maxwell, a nature enthusiast, during a walk in Holyrood Park, near Salisbury Crags, Edinburgh. After he spotted the distinctive-looking spider, which has a white V-shape on its black back, experts confirmed the species type.

Spurred on by this success, Mr Maxwell began searching in similar habitat near Calton Hill, where he discovered the *Sitticus pubescens*.

Now arachnologists and conservationists will work to ensure the future of the tiny creatures, which grow to only seven millimetres in length and are more commonly found in southern England. While they are at a loss to explain their appearance in Edinburgh, many believe they might always have been there but had been undetected until now.

Both arachnids belong to the same family as the common zebra spider – named after its eye-catching black and white striped body – which can be seen in many gardens throughout Scotland.

Mr Maxwell, 34, said: 'It is exciting. I was out with my video camera on Arthur's Seat a few weeks ago and spotted an unusual-looking spider and got it on tape. I showed it to experts and they confirmed what it was.

'I then went to look at another site and that's where I discovered the second rare species. It is just something I do in my spare time but it is satisfying when something like this happens.'

Jim Stewart, the principal spider recorder for Edinburgh with the Lothian Wildlife Information Centre, said: 'These are highly significant discoveries and all thanks to the keen eyesight of Mr Maxwell. It is good to find these new species, especially when they have only been previously sighted in areas far away from Edinburgh and so long ago.'

Bob Saville, of the information centre, which is operated by the Scottish Wildlife Trust, said: 'This is very exciting news, although it is a mystery as to why we are suddenly finding these species but that is part of the fascination about this kind of work.

'There are so many creatures out there and so few people actually looking for them,' he added.

The spider *Aelurillus v-insignatus* is now expected to be added to the Edinburgh Biodiversity Action Plan, which records the key species of wildlife in the capital and aims to protect habitats.

David Jamieson, landscape and nature conservation officer with the City of Edinburgh Council, said: 'This is a significant find and it will be added to our list of 100 species which we are in the process of drawing up action plans for.'

The Scotsman, 20 August 1998

Topic 6 extracts 2 and 3

Rare butterfly back after 100 years

Grayling: *Breeding site secrecy*

Robert McNeil

Grayling butterflies have been found in Edinburgh for the first time in more than 100 years, breeding on railway tracks at several sites. Railtrack Scotland is keeping the locations secret so that collectors do not trespass on potentially dangerous lines.

A spokeswoman described the butterfly as 'this most welcome of rail travellers'.

The grayling usually lives on the coast, nesting on grassy slopes at the top of cliffs. The last recorded sighting in Edinburgh was in Morningside in 1894. The only other place in Scotland it can be found is at St Abb's Head, near Eyemouth. Last night a spokesman for the Scottish Wildlife Trust, whose members discovered the butterfly on the railway, expressed delight at its reappearance. 'It is great. We have to be a bit concerned about the effects of oil from the trains, but it is good news overall,' he said.

He said the butterflies may be taking to railway sites because they could lay their eggs in the embankments and then sun-bathe around the rails … but preferably not on them.

The Scotsman, 3 August 1996

Action to save forest ants

An action plan has been drawn up to protect a threatened species of ant that inhabits Scotland's Caledonian forests.

The Scottish Wildlife Trust is drawing up a programme to save the rare woodland ant, *Formica exsecta*. The narrow-headed insect is found only in Speyside and the lowland heaths of Devon. Habitat destruction has led to the disappearance of the ant from 70 per cent of English sites in the last 30 years. The Trust says urgent action is needed to ensure the insect's survival north of the border. In Scotland the largest populations are found on Speyside, in the forests of Glenmore, Rothiemurchus and Abernethy.

The UK has more than 40 species of ant but only five of those are wood ants. The long-legged ant builds labyrinthine nests with characteristic mounds. A study last year found that Glenmore Forest contains more nests than any other UK site, but the ant was absent from large areas of surrounding forest.

The Scotsman, 11 April 1998

WRITING AND SOLO TALK

Teachers' introduction

As with discussion, this unit does not teach teachers how to teach non-fiction writing or solo talk – skills that they have been teaching for years. It merely offers a way to draw a thread from one skill to another based on material provided. The teacher will need to revise non-fiction writing and solo talk in terms that the class is familiar with, before embarking on biodiversity solo talk and writing.

Pupils' introduction

When a person has a point to make, he or she can speak it or write it down. No matter which medium (writing or speaking) he or she chooses to use, the text has to be organised.

Both talking and writing non-fiction are organised in the same way.

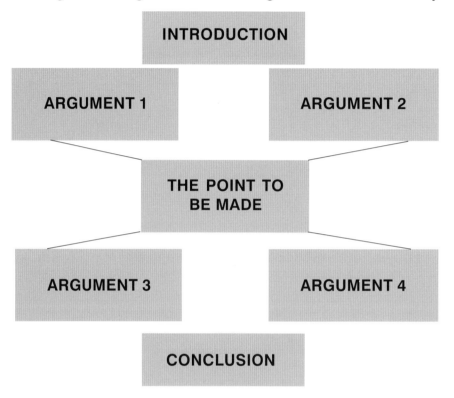

This simple diagram shows clearly how to construct a piece of non-fiction.

Step 1
Decide your point.

Step 2
Organise your arguments into sections and make note of the details in each box.

Step 3
Decide the order of your arguments, and provide link sentences and words.

Step 4
Write the introduction and the conclusion, perhaps as a pair.

(Note: all the articles in the Reading section and in the Talk (discussion) section follow this formula.)

Look back at a reading or a discussion article and identify:
- the introduction
- the arguments
- the link sentences and words
- the conclusion.

Introductory writing exercise

Using the ideas you gained in the discussion sessions, set a question for writing and another for solo talk and prepare them according to the box plan on page 148. This could be either a discursive essay or a non-fiction piece of writing.

Report writing

Teachers' introduction

Although report writing is no longer obligatory at Higher, and does not itself have a place at Standard Grade, it is a skill worth teaching in S4. Pupils can use report writing for their Writing 1, will still be able to do it at Higher, can use it in other subjects and in Higher Education, and are likely to require the skills at some point in life. Report writing also includes the inherent skills of selecting and rewriting, both of which are necessary for close reading. It is possible to teach report writing at all three levels, provided the language of the source material is suited to the reading abilities of the pupils. The text on pp. 155–158 outlines a suggested method of teaching report writing at all three levels, and then the material that follows is at different reading levels to suit students' abilities. Note that the step-by-step guide to report writing is modelled on one piece of writing, which is at lower General level. This allows all students, with support, to grasp the process being undertaken. They then carry this out at their own level. Before tackling the work, the extracts from *Biodiversity in Scotland* (pp. 151–154) should be read with the class, by way of:

* introducing the material
* pointing out non-fiction writing
* checking that pupils are reading with understanding.

SCOTLAND'S BIODIVERSITY: OUR NATURAL INHERITANCE

A brief history

Scotland's dramatic natural landscapes are the product of both natural forces and human activities. The indented coastline which breaks up to the north and west into islands, the mountains, carved gullies and boulder-strewn moors are legacies of a past ice age. Sculpted and eroded by ice, water and wind, the land was at first colonised by arctic wildlife. Remnants from this period still cling to existence in the high places and colder neuks of Scotland.

For a time as the climate warmed, an extensive mixed woodland of oak, birch, hazel, elm and Scots pine covered most of Scotland. For more than 6000 years, the Highlands and Islands were covered by 1.5 million hectares of wild wood.

A shift towards cooler and wetter weather, coupled with increasing human activity from the Middle Ages meant that swathes of the ancient forest were cleared and did not regenerate. After centuries of clearing, only 1% of the original forest was left. Trees gave way to grass and heather moorland. Peat bogs formed when layers of dead vegetation failed to decompose in cold and waterlogged conditions. Heavy demands for timber during two world wars and the grazing of new growth by sheep and red deer threatened even these remaining patches of forest with extinction.

In the latter half of this century, Scotland's patterns of land use changed again with much moorland, blanket bog and rough grassland being claimed for pasture, cereal crops and commercial forestry.

Modern Scotland enjoys or endures a cool, wet, maritime climate. This gives us, especially along the west coast, the richest collections of mosses and liverworts anywhere in the world.

Touching Shetland and sweeping down into the North Sea, the arctic waters bring northern marine species to our shores and influence the climate of the Highlands and Northern Isles. The combination of islands at a northern latitude with arctic influences means that Scotland has a diversity and total number of species which has much in common with Denmark, Norway and Sweden.

More than half of Scotland's land area is mountainous, including the highest ranges in the British Isles. The high lands are home to mosses and lichens, to rare plants like the oblong woodsia fern and alpine sow-thistle, and to birds like the ptarmigan, dotterel and snow bunting. Along the west, the comparative warmth of the North Atlantic Drift brings southern marine species occasionally to our coasts, like the leatherback turtle, sun fish and trigger fish.

Set on the north-western fringe of continental Europe and shielded from extremes of temperature by the warmish waters of the Gulf Stream and the prevailing westerly air flow, Scotland is a resting point for migratory birds travelling from colder winter climates. Many species of bird and fish return each year to their breeding grounds in Scotland, while other species, like geese, return to overwinter here from their breeding grounds in Greenland or Iceland.

Including its surrounding seas, Scotland has about 90,000 species of all forms of life. Some of our species are northern species existing at the southernmost tip of their ranges, and could disappear from Scotland if the climate becomes warmer. A number are southern species, found at the northern limits of their range – including bats, moths, flowering plants and some liverworts – and could correspondingly extend northwards in a warmer climate.

Scotland's biodiversity (continued)

The number of species living in and around Scotland, from the approximate 12-mile limit in the sea to the tops of the mountains.

Group	Number of species
Single-celled organisms (including viruses, bacteria and protozoa)	c. 44,100
Fungi (including lichens)	c. 9,140
Plants (including algae, mosses, ferns and flowering plants)	c. 11,000
Invertebrate animals (including slugs and snails, sea shells, starfish, worms of all kinds, sponges, insects, spiders and mites)	c. 24,800
Fish (both fresh- and sea-water)	244
Amphibians (frog, toads and newts)	6
Reptiles (lizards, snake and turtle)	4
Birds	242
Mammals (including whales and dolphins)	63
Total	c. 89,600

Usher, M. B., Scotland's 'Biodiversity: an overview', in *Biodiversity in Scotland: Status, Trends and Initiatives*, L.V. Fleming et al. (eds), Edinburgh: The Stationery Office, 1997, pp. 5–20

Why should we value it?

The biodiversity around us is a life-support system for our planet, and helps to sustain human life. Peat bogs lock up carbon dioxide – a greenhouse gas – and absorb impurities from rainwater, filtering pure water through into Scotland's salmon and trout rivers. Beds of kelp and other seaweeds absorb the force of waves, reducing coastal erosion. The tiny plants that float in the top few metres of sea water absorb huge amounts of carbon dioxide, returning oxygen into the air.

From nature's store we take our food, fuel, clothing and construction materials. Much of Scotland's economy, particularly in rural areas, depends directly or indirectly on work that exploits our natural resources. Scotland's thriving whisky industry relies for its product on the contributions made by pure water and natural yeasts. In general, healthy environments help to attract visitors, and tourism in turn makes a significant contribution to many rural economies. Organisations that invest in Scotland benefit from Scotland's reputation for producing high quality goods from natural materials, and an ability to offer their employees a high quality of life in magnificent surroundings.

Many of our medicines originated with plants, and alternative therapies like herbalism, homoeopathy and aromatherapy also make use of natural materials. The search in the natural world for effective treatments for

Scotland's biodiversity (continued)

diseases like cancer, AIDS and the common cold continues.

Advances in genetic engineering have opened up new possibilities of breeding disease- and pest-resistant crops. Such discoveries often depend on close observation of naturally occurring processes, and on researchers having access to a range of naturally occurring chemicals and genetic sequences. Species and habitats which have evolved to their present state over thousands of years may be quickly lost and cannot then be recovered. Most losses are irreplaceable – like the peat bogs which formed over thousands of years, or the oil reserves beneath our seas. In preserving the natural world we are keeping our options open for the future.

The world around us also inspires and invigorates us. It feeds into our culture, storytelling and legends, informs our designs and architecture and echoes within our literature and music. It is Scotland's natural heritage, and it concerns us all.

Influenced by people

An estimated 99% of Scotland's land bears the marks of human activities. Parts of the sea bed around Scotland's coast are disturbed by fishing nets and dredgers many times a year, and scientists do not yet know the effects of this intrusion on settled sea-bed communities. Some Scottish habitats, like the machair of the Western Isles and heather moorland, have been formed largely by human management and depend for their continuing diversity of species on the long-established practices of grazing, cultivation and occasional burning that helped to create them.

Our use of Scotland's land, fresh and coastal waters has changed over the centuries, and changed rapidly during this century.

Prompted by emerging technologies and the drive for a higher material standard of living, our consumption of natural resources has become much more aggressive. Agriculture is more intensive and specialised, and as a consequence the total variety of species the land can support has reduced. Pollution, both localised and diffuse, is detectable in our groundwater, rivers and seas. There are fears for the future survival of certain marine species, and the use of longer nets and powerful winches mean that we are harvesting species of fish from the deep oceans that scientists have not yet had the opportunity to study. Non-native and invasive species like rhododendron and giant hogweed have been introduced or encroached into established habitats, diminishing the range of fungi, insects, animals and flowering plants they can support.

We change our environment when we interact with it. Some changes can bring unforeseen consequences. Others may subtly alter the natural balance, creating changes that may not easily be noticed until the position becomes irretrievable.

To protect our environment, we must understand it better. In some cases, scientific research has demonstrated that our current practices are not sustainable. In others, we have been able to use improved understanding of some species to provide a better environment, and many kinds of seabirds and birds of prey are increasing in number. Conservation is by no means confined to the remote places of Scotland. In the urban and suburban areas, studies are being made of the plants, animals and microbes around us, and a greater awareness of them allows us to co-exist with them.

We have the ability to influence our environment significantly, for better or worse, and we have a responsibility to use it wisely.

Scotland's biodiversity (continued)

Changing habitats

Blanket bog

Scotland has over 70% of all bog peat in Great Britain. These are natural archives, strong information in layers of peat about the plant and animal life of the past 3000–7000 years. They also support a variety of plants and animals which have adapted to this environment – like sphagnum moss, which grows in nitrogen-poor soils and is mainly responsible for the continued bog growth, and the common sundew, a carnivorous plant that catches insects to provide it with the nutrients lacking in the bog. The high water content of bogs makes them an ideal environment for wading birds, and for many birds of prey. There are concerns about the future of Scotland's blanket bog. Some has been lost to conifer woodland or drained to provide rough pasture. Parts are eroding and losing surface vegetation, probably through a combination of grazing, burning and weather. The remainder is also vulnerable to chemical changes, becoming more acid through pollution from the air. Scotland has one of the richest concentrations of blanket bog in Europe, and the Flow Country of Caithness and Sutherland is probably the largest single expanse of blanket bog in the world. How can we best protect this distinctive habitat?

Mountain vegetation

Scotland's mountains are relatively unspoilt, and support many rare and unusual plants and upland birds. Like the bogs, the uplands are threatened by chemical pollution from the air which damages vulnerable plants like the mosses. Grazing sheep and deer are cropping vegetation to the roots, damaging the plants and the birds, like the dotterel, that nest among them. Hillwalkers may also be contributing to the erosion of mountain soils, and the processes of erosion are little understood.

Biodiversity in Scotland, The Scottish Biodiversity Group, 1997

Pupils' notes

This unit of work involves writing a report based on a range of available material. You will be given three or four items of text and a report writing task. In each case, what you have to do is:
- *select* the relevant parts of the material to fit your task
- *reorganise* that material into the box plan (see Pupils' introduction to Writing and Solo Talk section, p. 148)
- *write* the report as a non-fiction essay.

There are certain rules.

- You cannot use speech.
- You cannot use headings.
- You cannot copy out large sections of the original.
- You must write in your own words.

To give you an idea of how to go about report writing, read the passage on the red squirrel and the step-by-step instructions that follow, and use this as a practice example.

Red squirrel loses more ground to grey invader

By Charles Clover, Environment Editor

The red squirrel is believed to have become extinct in one of its last remaining English strongholds as a result of competition with the introduced American grey.

The Wildlife trusts say that there has been no reliable sighting of the red squirrel around Cannock Chase, Staffs, since 1994.

Meanwhile, the trusts warn that battle lines are being redrawn in the north-east of England where the grey squirrel is advancing into Northumberland along the Derwent valley and into the Tyne valley.

Debby Smith, who began studying squirrels on Cannock Chase in 1993, said: 'When I started the project, we still had red squirrels on Cannock Chase. Although I can't be 100 per cent certain that there are no reds, my work is now confined to studying the ecology of grey squirrels in plantations.'

Isobel Bretherton, of the trusts' national office, said: 'People like to think that they have seen a red squirrel but what they have seen is a grey squirrel with reddish hair. No knowledgeable naturalist has seen a red on Cannock Chase since 1994.'

Miss Smith, who has had support from Staffordshire Wildlife trust, the Forestry Commission and English Nature, said it was now thought that simple competition for food rather than direct aggression had pushed out the reds. Greys live at higher densities and compete for food.

She said: 'Eventually the greys outcompete the reds. The reds will move to get food and if there isn't anywhere to go, they'll die.'

They grey squirrel now numbers 2.5 million nationwide since a handful were introduced to Britain from North America in 1876. There are now only 160,000 red squirrels, mostly in isolated populations. Three quarters of the national population of reds is in Scotland.

Greys have a more varied diet, being able to digest unripe nuts and seeds whereas reds have difficulty living off a diet mainly consisting of acorns and prefer the seeds of conifers. Greys are immune to the parapox virus which wipes out reds equal to years of their rivals colonising an area.

There are some reds in Thetford Chase on the Norfolk Suffolk border, in Lancashire, on islands in Poole Harbour, Dorset, and on the Isle of Wight. But the strongholds in England remain in Durham and Cumbria.

Lisa Kerslake, of the Northumberland and Durham Wildlife Trust's Red Alert Project, said: ' There are still lots of reds in the Tyne valley. Obviously we are worried but it is only a matter of time before that changes. You need a hard front line.'

Durham Wildlife Trust has teamed up with local authorities, the Woodland Trust and land managers to trap greys in the 'red-only' zone.

A survey carried out by Lord Joicey, a trust member, found that greys had been infil-trating 'red' zones, moving northwards from Durham, southwards from Scotland and spreading along the River Tweed.

Viscount Ridley, who has reds on his Blagdon estate near Newcastle, is chairman of the Red Alert panel and has per-suaded many land owners to trap greys.

The Daily Telegraph, 7 January 1998

If you had been set the task of writing a report on the causes of the changing animal population of Britain, you might have had as one of your sources of material the article that you have just read. What you would have to do with it is as follows.

Step 1
Make sure you are clear about the purpose of your report. In this case it is to write about the causes of the changing animal population in Britain. It is important to keep the purpose of the writing in mind.

Step 2
Read the passage through again highlighting or underlining *the main points that fit the purpose of the report.*

Step 3
Write brief notes on the points you have underlined, for example, red squirrels becoming extinct because grey squirrels:
- compete for food
- have a more varied diet
- are immune to a virus that attacks red squirrels.

Step 4
Decide whether you want to use any of the quotes. As you are not allowed to use speech, you must rewrite the words in to *indirect speech*. An example makes this clear. The original text contains the *direct speech*:

Lisa Kerslake of the Northumberland and Durham Wildlife Trusts' Red Alert project said: 'There are still lots of reds in the Tyne valley. Obviously we are worried that it is only a matter of time before that changes. You need a hard front line.'

In indirect speech, this could be:

Conservationists are afraid that red squirrels in many areas will be destroyed, and feel that serious measures need to be taken.

Step 5
Any other articles supplied as part of the source material need to be tackled in a similar way to that outlined for the red squirrels article (steps 2–4).

Step 6
Plan the report using the box plan in the Pupils' introduction to the Writing and Solo Talk section (p. 148). Organise the material you wish

to use from all the articles you have, by putting together the information on the same topics, that is, all the material on:
- competition for food
- different diet
- virus.

Step 7
Write your report.

Foundation report writing

Report writing on items F1–F4

Using items F1, F2, F3 and F4, write a report on the effects that the damage to forests, trees and mountains has on people. At the end of your report, suggest what we should do about this.

Base your writing entirely on the texts provided. Your report should be about 150 words.

Item F1

VANISHING MOUNTAINS

Mountain ecosystems are suffering from soil erosion, landslides and the rapid loss of animals and plant life.

Agenda 21, chapter 13

Mountains are more than just huge rocks decorated with snow. They are homes to whole communities of plants and animals which depend on them for life. When mountain forests are chopped down, these communities crumble away with the earth beneath them. Earth exposed in the wake of deforestation is washed away by rains.

Mountains are vital for more than half the people of the planet who live in the shadow of water or climate systems that flow down from them. If the people and life systems which grow on mountains are vanishing we are under threat.

COMMUNITY EROSION

When rain forests are cut down on mountain sides and the earth is washed away, new trees find it hard to grow in the remaining soil. There are landslides and loss of homes for animals. Native people who have lived for centuries in the mountains also lose their livelihoods. They are forced to move to nearby cities to find work. The younger generation, ignorant of mountain traditions, do not learn from their grandparents how to look after their fragile ecosystems.

> **Malawi**
>
> In my country, people in the mountains are so desperate to find land to cultivate, they tie ropes round their waists and hang off mountain sides to dig the ground and plant seeds. Of course, after a couple of harvests, the good ground falls away leaving behind bare rock.
>
> *Benji, 14, Malawi*

Rescue Mission Planet Earth

Item F2

CHAINSAW MASSACRE

Forests worldwide are now threatened by uncontrolled exploitation by human beings. They are being turned into farms or destroyed for timber and other uses.

Agenda 21, chapter 11

A forest is more than a neat arrangement of matchsticks. In the Amazon rain forest, a scientist found that a single tree provides a home for two thousand unique species of animals. Forests are vital to our global ecosystems: they act as sinks for carbon dioxide. Rip them away and humans could not survive. In many countries, especially developing ones, forests are vital to the larger social and economic picture: millions of trees are cut down every year in the name of survival. Logging, agriculture, fire, acid rain - all conspire to destroy forests. But in the tropical rain forests - it's a massacre.

Ragamuffin Nature, Tink again
All de people man dem, tink again
before burning down de forest, tink again
to build de house man, tink again
before to cut de trees man, tink again

Tink all da people or some o dem
once de forest will go
de desert will come again
As de increase in a de CO2 will make de
world hotter so making life some shorter

Man me say tink again, tink about de
desert de oxygen and de flower
All de people me say loudly, tink again
Amish K. Shah, Tanzania

Rescue Mission Planet Earth

Item F2 (continued)

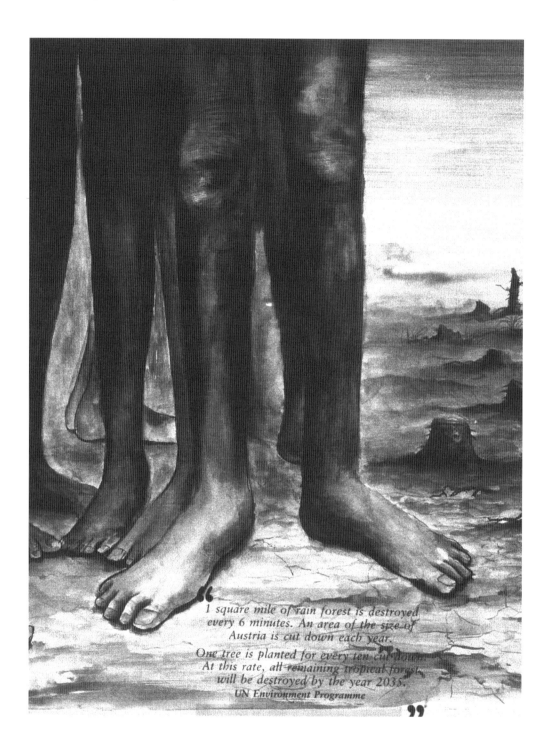

Rescue Mission Planet Earth
© Peace Child International 1994. Reproduced by permission of
Kingfisher Publications plc. All rights reserved.

Item F3

SEA OF TROUBLES

Oceans are under increasing stress from pollution, over-fishing and general degradation. It affects everything from the climate to coral reefs. Agenda 21, chapter 17

Our seas are under intense pressure from pollution, most of which comes from human beings. Like the atmosphere, it is incredibly flexible, but we are pushing it to its limits. It's going to get worse: by the year 2020, three-quarters of us will be living 60km (40 miles) from a coastline. If we don't change, those extra people will be pouring sewage and waste into the seas.

600,000 tons of oil is junked into the sea by ships every year as a matter of course! No wonder many of the fish we are catching are unfit to eat. That doesn't stop us trying to catch them. Some use huge, mile-long drift nets that catch dolphins and other things we don't need. Over-fishing means worldwide fish catches are dropping.

Harri Sara & Antte Aarnio, Finland

Hong Kong

Bathing in the sea now is not a pleasure at all in Hong Kong. Untreated sewage is constantly found in seas. Visitors have to reluctantly keep away and swim in pools instead.

The water quality in Rambler Channel is getting worse at an alarming rate. There's zero oxygen in the water and a lot of mud contaminated mud poisonous metals....

Red tides off the East Coast of Hong Kong are killing hundreds of fish. Red tides are big plumes of algae, the stuff that turns ponds and rivers green. In the sea, it's a rust red colour, not poisonous, but it sucks oxygen out of the water and kill tons of fish and seals. In Hong Kong, they are killing all the fish in the fish farms. Bad for business.

Livingstone School, Hong Kong

Rescue Mission Planet Earth

Item F3 (continued)

The Mermaids
I saw the mermaids
Crawl up on the shore
They couldn't live longer
Down there any more

They had horrible stories
Of what's going on there
The scenes that they witnessed
Which they couldn't bear

They told of a black cloud
That sometimes spread on top
From which strange black rain
Towards them did drop

They also saw huge nets
Rumbling in the deep
Dragging all inside them
Big and small fish to keep.
                    Dorothy Sciberras, Malta

Rescue Mission Planet Earth

Item F4

PLANT RICHES

- Many medicines were originally derived from plants. Aspirin, for example, was developed from a chemical extracted from meadowsweet, and, even today, million of sufferers from heart disease owe their lives to chemicals extracted from the dried leaves of foxgloves.
- More recently, chemicals extracted from the rosy periwinkle, a rare flowering plant from Madagascar, have been shown to slow or control the development of childhood leukaemia. In 1987, scientists discovered that a chemical extracted from the Moreton Bay chestnut, an uncommon Australian tree, reacts with the virus that causes AIDS, and research is continuing into its potential as a treatment for this disease.
- Most species have never been screened for their medicinal value, yet huge numbers of species are in danger of extinction. Unless we can protect them from this fate, the riches stored in their cell will be lost for ever.
- Even where we grow plants as crops, we are losing the biodiversity *within* the species, by constantly selecting seed from plants which produce the highest yeilds. This is reducing the species' capacity to cope with change, yet that natural adaptability could become very important to us in the future if "Global Warming" drastically changes the climate in which crops grow. And of course the value of conserving biodiversity within domesticated animal species is also increasingly recognised, as work with rare agricultural breeds shows.

The poster illustrates the scientific link between jellyfish and cancer cells. In 1996, scientists announced that they had found ways of using the natural light-emitting chemicals produced by a species of jellyfish – possibly to attract its prey at night – as markers to pinpoint cancer cells in the human body, helping them in their search for a cure for cancers.

BIODIVERSITY VALUES

why does biodiversity matter?

- The new concept of 'biodiversity' has helped provide a focus to concentrate minds on the value of the living world to our lives. And biodiversity is something that matters to everyone in Scotland, whether they live on Papa Stour or in Castlemilk.
- A recent article in *The Scotsman* summarised the value of biodiversity thus:-
- "Biodiversity controls the tapestry of life. It is what colours the landscape and gives Scotland its unique scenic qualities. That makes it a key asset of the Scottish tourism industry, equal in importance with our historical and cultural heritage.
- "Biodiversity helpes soften the artificiality of city life – a garden, after all, is just a carefully structured haven of biodiversity. Biodiversity gives the fisherman his living, and lies at the heart of successful farming and forestry. And if we fail to protect biodiversity, they will be among the first to suffer.
- "Biodiversity is therefore a key element in all our lives, and the need to protect it impinges on almost every aspect of our society."
- That does not even mention the future, unknown values that may still await us, but which we risk losing unless we protect our living heritage of biodiversity.

...portant that ...cies like the Soay Sheep are conserved.
Laurie Campbell

biodiversity quotes

- "Besides the profound ethical and aesthetic implications, it is clear that the loss of biodiversity has serious economic and social costs. The genes, species, ecosystems and human knowledge which are being lost represent a living library of options available for adapting to local and global change. Biodiversity is part of our daily lives and livelihoods, and constitutes the resources upon which families, communities, nations and future generations depend."
  ELISABETH DOWDESWELL Executive Director, United Nations Environment Programme (in Introduction to Global Biodiversity Assessment)

Biodiversity publication, *The Variety of Life*, Scottish Natural Heritage/RSPB

Report writing on item F5

Using item F5, write a report on how people and animals can improve the environment. Your report should be about 150 words.

Item F5

OPERATION CLEANUP

Prevent or minimize the generation of waste. This should be part of an overall cleaner production approach; by 2010, all countries should have national plans for waste management.

Agenda 21, chapters 20 & 22

There is a clear solution to the waste problem: waste should not be produced in the first place. We've got used to waste as an inevitable fact of life but in fact waste is always a big mistake. Industry can and should introduce ways of making things without producing waste.

One of the interesting things happening on human settlements, is some wonderful work that has been done on the development of the indigenous materials for housing. We're actually creating housing materials from waste. This is being done in a number of countries - bricks made from waste are actually produced in different countries so we're creating new industries, jobs and so on as well as using up waste.

Elizabeth Dowdeswell, Under-Secretary-General
UNEP/HABITAT

WHAT CAN WE DO?
Do not create waste. Buy only things that you really need and things that last. When you can't make use of them any more, recycle or find another person who needs them.

Compost all your household waste; use a compost toilet to dispose of your sewage. Don't buy products that are wrapped in unnecessary, cute covers.

The most important thing is to pressure industry to move on to waste-free processes. Try to find out which companies are wasting what and let it influence your shopping decisions. Then boycott their products. When enough of us do that, they will have to change their ways.

AGENDA 21 SAYS:
• Reduce waste, recycle and tax packaging materials.
• Require that industry adopt cleaner production methods.
• Developed countries: promote the transfer of low-waste production methods to developing countries.
• Give the people the right to know the risks of chemicals they are exposed to.
• Immediately clean up contaminated areas and give help to their inhabitants.
• Make polluters pay cleanup costs.
• Ensure that the military disposes of their hazardous waste properly.
• Ban illegal export of hazardous waste to countries not equipped to deal with it.
• Minimize creation of radioactive waste.

Item F5 (continued)

EXPLOSION AT KLONG TOEY, 1991

One Saturday afternoon in March an unusual billowing cloud of smoke was seen hovering in the air. We all knew that Bangkok was polluted, but we never thought that it was that bad. There were chemicals in the air, in exposed food and water and in the blood of the residents of these areas.

The accident probably started when containers of phosporus ignited spontaneously in front of a warehouse, producing an intense fire which quickly consumed several warehouses.

It has left behind many serious problems - complaints of itchy skin, rashes, wounds that took place at the time and have never healed; pregnant women whose babies have died in the womb. To make matters worse many of the people fell ill.

The residents of the Klong Toey area are not aware how serious and toxic the explosion was. Although many were offered other temporary housing they preferred to remain where they were. Those whose homes were destroyed wanted to rebuild their shacks over the burnt and contaminated area.

After the explosion, jerrycans, drums and plastic bags containing lethal chemicals, acids that survived the fire were stacked all over the surrounding areas. Despite warnings on the containers - to keep these materials in cool temperatures, out of direct sunlight - they were left unprotected, directly in the sun. The result was fire. Warnings about not using these cans to extinguish fire were totally ignored.

Another problem was that many large amounts of chemicals stored in Klong Toey ports were unlabelled. More than 50 % of chemical cargo kept in the Port Authority of Thailand warehouses were moved out of the Klong Toey port area during the following weeks. Nobody knows where they went.

It seems to me, that government officials in Bangkok don't want to take responsibility for such problems when they occur. The result is confusion about "it's someone else's responsibility." Many people knew the chemicals were being stored under wrong conditions but because of this "May-pen-rai" (never mind) attitude, Thai residents suffered. We hope that the Thai government learnt a lesson from this horrible experience. In the short term they need to look at relocation and housing assistance for the people who lived in the Klong Toey area. The government could move the people out of Bangkok to start a housing program on less expensive land. They could then provide free transportation for their jobs in the city. They have started to clean up the Klong Toey slum, although this is more due to pressure from citizens that government efficiency.

For the future, the government must prevent this sort of problem happening again. Inexpensive health care and housing programs need to be started for the poor, possibly through taxes and donations. There should also be better enviromental education for the whole community through schools, newspapers and television. There is a TV program once a week which informs people of the enviromental problems being faced in Thailand. This is the step in the right direction.

Lalana Panijpan, 18, Thailand

General report writing

Report writing on items G1–G4

Using items G1, G2, G3 and G4, write a report on the increase of almost-extinct animals. You should:
- deal with the main points about the increase in numbers
- explain the value of this.

Your report should be about 300 words long and be based only on material in the sources provided.

Item G1

Bid to welcome back the beaver

The beaver could soon be heading back to Scotland, writes *Elizabeth Buie*, Environment Correspondent.

Areas around the Ness, Spey, Tay, Dee, Don and Loch Lomond could be populated by about 1000 within the next 50 years if there is public support for a proposal by the Government's conservation agency, Scottish Natural Heritage.

SNH chairman Magnus Magnusson yesterday launched a consultation exercise to gauge public feeling on a plan to bring back the European beaver, hunted to death in Scotland 400 years ago.

'We felt that restoring this missing element in our biodiversity would bring real benefits to the ecology of our rivers and lochs and would also benefit local economies from increased wildlife tourism,' he said.

Between six and 10 could be introduced every year beginning in 2001, with the target of about 1000 by 2050. They would probably have to be imported from Scandinavia at about £1000 each.

There was concern that their reintroduction after such a long absence would have an adverse impact on fishing and forestry, but SNH scientists argued that in contrast to its 'lumberjack' American cousin, often regarded as a pest, the European beaver could play a major role in revitalising the ecology of Scotland's waters.

The Herald, 20 March 1998

Item G2

Pine martens fight back from the brink of extinction

By Dani Garavelli

The pine marten, once hunted to near extinction in its native Scotland, is on the march and moving south from its Highland stronghold to begin to colonise the central belt and even further south into England and Wales.

The cat-sized carnivores, with a taste for rabbits, squirrels and pheasants, are feared by gamekeepers because of their reputation as killing machines. The Victorians all but wiped them out by trapping, shooting and poisoning but the advent of commercial forestry plantations provided a belated sanctuary for a handful of the animals.

The species was put on the protected list in 1988. Ten years later, however, its recovery has been spectacular and there is now believed to a population of around 2,500. They mainly live in Perthshire in the east and on the Kintyre peninsula in the west. Isolated animals have been found in Northumberland and north Wales.

'The resurgence of the pine marten is creating problems for gamekeepers. An agile creature, it can bypass many sophisticated security measures to reach its prey. Some keepers are already thought to be taking the law into their own hands by setting illegal traps to prevent colonies being established in their areas, but others are looking at ways of resolving the conflict so pine martens and pheasants can share the countryside.

Keepers on four Highland estates have been working with researcher Elizabeth Balharry, of the Vincent Wildlife Trust, in a scheme to test the effectiveness of electric fences for keeping pine martens in check. Mike Watt, on the Scatwell estate near Inverness, was one of those who took part – largely, he admits, because he was worried by the rising number of pheasant losses over the past five years as the pine marten population has grown.

'I accept that animals kill to eat, it is the way of the countryside,' he said. 'But when pine martens get into a release pen they go into a killing frenzy. At the peak of the season, the losses can be very high, so we have to do something to protect the birds.

'Working with Elizabeth allowed us to test various ways of using electric fences to keep the pine martens out. Eventually we came up with a version involving an overhang, which seemed to work well, and, as a result, we had no pheasant losses last year. Setting it up did involve more work, but it was worth it.'

The Vincent Wildlife Trust has now launched a major publicity drive, distributing leaflets through the Game Conservancy Trust and the British Association for Shooting and Conservation in an attempt to raise awareness about the pine marten.

English Nature is also about to publish a consultation document on the possible reintroduction of the pine marten into southern England using animals from the strongest Scottish colonies.

A female pine marten and her young in a birch wood in north-west Scotland are to feature in a *Wildlife on One* programme on BBC1 on Tuesday. It is narrated by David Attenborough.

Manuel Hinge, who filmed the programme, said: 'It was very difficult as pine martens are nocturnal and elusive. But they are real characters.

'It is true that they attack species such as capercaillies and red squirrels which are in decline, but those species also face other threats such as motor cars and the destruction of their habitats.'

Scotland on Sunday, 5 April 1998

Item G3

Shark can bask in safety as it joins new protected list

By Charles Clover, Environment Editor

The basking shark, the bluebell and the water vole were among 35 species protected or given added protection by the Government yesterday following the biggest review of the threats to rare wildlife for five years.

It will now become illegal to kill, injure, disturb or sell the basking shark, the second largest fish in the world, together with the twaite shad, giant goby and *Clavopsella navis*, a marine hydroid three millimetres long and found only in a Sussex lagoon.

It will also become illegal to sell stag beetles or wild bluebells or to disturb the bankside habitat of the water vole, the fastest-declining British mammal – largely thanks to American mink.

Legal protection has been increased for the allis shad, marsh fritillary butterfly, large copper butterfly and the pearl mussel.

The pearl mussel received immediate protection from sale – it was already illegal to kill or injure it while hunting for pearls – because of the grim state of the mussel population and fears that mussel beds will be plundered this spring. The other species will be protected from 16 April. Convictions under the Wildlife and Countryside Act carry fines of up to £5,000.

The hedgehog fungus, a species confined to the New Forest, where it grows on decaying beech trees, is one of four fungi to receive full protection for the first time. Also protected are the sandy stilt puffball, now confined to a handful of Suffolk road verges where it is protected by wildlife trusts and the county council, the royal bolete and oak polypore.

Other plants protected include the Deptford pink, dwarf spike rush, flamingo moss and polar feather-moss.

Altogether 11 species of animal and 17 species of plant were given protection for the first time under the Wildlife and Countryside Act. A further four species received enhanced protection. One species, the viper's bugloss moth, will be removed from the Wildlife and Countryside Act as it is now deemed to be extinct. Michael Meacher, the environment minister, said the decision to protect the basking shark, the second largest fish in the world after the whale shark, was intended to be 'exemplary' and because of the threatened status of the shark elsewhere in the world.

The basking shark is no longer killed in British waters – single fishermen in the Clyde used to harpoon them until two years ago and Gavin Maxwell, the author of *Ring of Bright Water*, built up a fishery for basking sharks off the west of Scotland in the 1950s – but there has been a fear that someone might start again.

Norway kills about 300 basking sharks in the north-east Atlantic each year but not enough is known about the basking shark to tell if these are from the declining population around Britain.

The dried fins of the basking shark are worth £80 a kilo in the markets of the Far East for shark's fin soup.

It now becomes illegal to trade in wild bluebells, after the Government accepted most of the recommendations of the Nature Conservation Committee for changes to the 1983 Act. Britain holds 20 per cent of the world's population of bluebells.

Until now it has been legal to harvest bluebells with the permission of the landowner, but wild bluebells are threatened by a bulb trade estimated to be worth £1 million a year. Those convicted of selling wild bluebells will now be liable to fines of up to £2,500.

The Wildlife Trusts welcomed the changes to the law protecting the basking shark and the bluebell, as these were threatened by killing, collection and trade.

But it said the public should not be fooled into thinking that most species were 'saved' since loopholes in the Wildlife and Countryside Act prevented the protection of their habitat from incidental damage by legitimate agricultural operations.

Item G3 (continued)

Simon Lyster, the Trusts' director-general, said: 'For others such as the marsh fritillary butterfly it will make little difference. The reason is that agriculture is swallowing up unimproved grassland where its food plant is found.'

The stag beetle, which had declined because of the increasing tidiness of woodland and lack of dead wood where its larvae grow, can now no longer be sold. Collection for sale on the continent is thought to be a contributory factor in its demise.

The Daily Telegraph, 27 March 1998; © Telegraph Group Limited, 2000

Item G4

The poster shows bog moss (Sphagnum sp.). Beneath the surface of the bog, its dead, partially decayed remains form the peat that covers vast areas of Scotland. These peatlands act as natural water filters. The clean rivers arising from them are essential for the survival of salmon – and of the salmon angling industry which contributes £70 million a year to the Scottish economy.

RETURNING TO ROOTS

Until recent decades, agriculture relied on natural ecosystem processes for its productivity. Soil fertility was maintained by the rotation of crops, with fallow periods in which 'weed' species with nitrogen-fixing bacteria in their roots were encouraged, and rich farm manure was spread over fields to restore nutrients and humus to the soil.

In the search for higher yields, farmers have turned increasingly to chemical fertilisers, produced by energy-intensive industries which boost greenhouse gases in the atmosphere and rapidly consume mineral resources. The intensive use of chemicals has threatened farmland ecosystems, disrupting natural balances and allowing some species to proliferate as pests.

Increasingly, people are questioning the wisdom of this "industrial farming". Less intensive, organic farming is being valued more highly. The economic and ecological consequences of high levels of chemical use are being recognised, and there is renewed interest in low-input farming. Scottish Natural Heritage has been assisting this work with its TIBRE (Targeted Inputs for a Better Rural Environment) project, which is investigating how new technology and products can make farming more environmentally friendly while retaining profitability.

ECOSYSTEM SERVICES

the value of ecosystems

- All the plants and animals living together in an area interact in a complex way with one another, and with the physical environment around them, and this intermeshing living system is called an ecosystem.
- Ecosystems maintain natural plant and animal communities, but they also provide benefits to human society. For example, natural vegetation helps maintain the balance of gases in the atmosphere, by releasing oxygen and absorbing carbon dioxide, one of the main 'greenhouse gases'. Healthy, growing vegetation therefore has a vital role in slowing the build up of these gases in the atmosphere from human industries, and so helps to reduce the potential scale of climate change (or global warming). Peatlands also act as an important 'sink' for greenhouse gases, and their destruction is accelerating the pace of climate change.
- Natural ecosystems regulate the release of water into the air (thus moderating rainfall), into the soil, and into burns and rivers (thus helping to control floods and reduce droughts). Healthy riverbank woodland further limits the risk of flooding – with all the destruction and economic loss it brings – and maintains water quality. Similarly, coastal sand-dune and saltmarsh ecosystems help protect the coastline.

biodiversity quotes

- "The mere phrase 'ecosystem services' has a mundane ring, rather like waste disposal or water quality control. But if only a small percentage of the journeyman organisms filling these roles were to disappear, human life would be diminished and strikingly less pleasant. It is a failing of our species that we ignore and even despise the creatures whose lives sustain our own."
  EDWARD WILSON, *The Diversity of Life* (1992).

Biodiversity publication, *The Variety of Life*, Scottish Natural Heritage/RSPB

Report writing on items G5–G7

Using items G5, G6 and G7, write a report on the damaging behaviour of the human race.

Base it entirely on the material provided and write not more than 300 words.

Item G5

Deadly inheritance

UKRAINE: Swallows reveal long-term impact of radioactive fall-out.

New research provides the strongest evidence yet that radioactive material released into the environment by the Chernobyl nuclear disaster has caused harmful mutations that are being passed from one generation to the next.

A team of scientists from Sweden and France compared the frequency of partial albinism, the loss of pigmentation caused by mutations in the DNA, in the plumage of swallows breeding in Chernobyl and in uncontaminated control areas. Albinism is bad news for swallows: birds affected are easily spotted by predators, and those that do survive are less likely to reproduce, finding it harder to attract a mate.

The scientists report (*Nature*, vol. 389, pp. 593–596) that about 15 per cent of birds bred in Chernobyl following the disaster in 1986 are partial albinos, compared to a frequency scarcely above 0 per cent in uncontaminated areas. This difference was not apparent in museum specimens collected from the same sites before 1986, showing that the condition is caused by the radioactive contamination.

Increases in the incidence of mutation-induced conditions such as thyroid cancer and infant leukaemia in humans have already been recorded from Chernobyl, but the latest study shows that the mutations are of a form which are likely to afflict the population for generations to come. There are two types of genetic mutation: somatic, which affects the individual with the condition but is not passed on to offspring, and germ line, which is carried in the eggs or sperm and so affects future generations.

'The swallow study demonstrates that these are germline mutations ... [which] was not the case in the other studies,' says Anders Møller of Université Pierre et Marie Curie in Paris, one of the scientists who carried out the work. While only 13 per cent of birds with normal parents were partial albino, 84 per cent of birds with partial albino parents were afflicted, showing that the mutation is heritable.

Furthermore, the scientists showed that the DNA structure was altered between parents and offspring in families of swallows breeding in Chernobyl but much less frequently uncontaminated areas, indicating a higher germ-line mutation rate in the former – 'the highest recorded mutation rate ever,' says Møller.

There is no reason to believe that swallows are particularly sensitive to radiation, especially since they only spend five months a year in the area. Indeed, according to Møller, 'working in Chernobyl was a little bit like *Silent Spring* – very few birds.' So the legacy of the worst ever nuclear accident may be a long one for many species of animals and plants, including humans.

Stuart Blackman, 'Deadly inheritance', *BBC Wildlife*, December 1997

Item G6

'The nightmare never ends'

INDONESIA: from orang-utans to insects, rainforest to coral reefs, the effects of the forest fires have, and will be, devastating.

The fax message pinned to the wall of the disaster centre in Jakarta is terse: 'Riau: Peat burning 6 m deep. Water shortages. Visibility 50 yards.' The bureaucrat shrugs. He has no resources and, even if 1,000 huge water-bombers flew in tomorrow, they couldn't put this lot out. 'The nightmare never ends,' he says, 'When will the rains come?'

The massive El Niño-induced drought that has settled on south-east Asia, providing tinder for one of the greatest fires on record, is the stuff of horror novels. Up to 25 million people across six countries have lived in a dangerously polluted atmosphere, many for up to six months. Almost two million hectares of secondary forest and scrubland has been consumed. Swamp forest, peatlands, wetlands, primary rainforest, coral and mangroves have all been affected. And the longer-term environmental effects are still being assessed.

The immediate effects of the fires and smoke are difficult to judge, too. More than 120 orang-utan are known to have come out of the forest, says Willie Smits, who runs the Wanariset Samboja conservatory in East Kalimantan. Many have been killed. 'Monkeys, Malayan sun bears, cobras, wild pigs and other animals come to the river to find cleaner air,' says the headman of Dadahuk village on the river Barito. 'Many are exhausted and the villagers kill them easily.' The forest is eerily silent in the smoke. There are no birds singing or amphibians calling.

The blazes have reached 16 protected areas. But smoke and soot may be having longer-term effects. By blotting out the sun and moon, and dropping temperatures up to 6 °C, flowering and fruiting has been set back. And, says Ron Lilley, of WWF Indonesia: 'All nectar-feeding insects, birds and bats will be affected if soot is deposited on flowers.'

The problem is that much of the land affected is already degraded, making it harder for nature to recover. If this were a one-off event, such as a hurricane or a volcano, it would not be so much of a problem.

But it is part of the chronic deterioration of ecosystems from overfishing, deforestation, logging and oil palm production.

Still unknown is the relationship between land and marine ecosystems. When the monsoons finally come, the run-off and soil erosion will be far greater than normal, and silt will be washed further out to sea. WWF expects corals and mangroves, which cannot tolerate sediment or fresh water, to be affected.

The worst news is that the fires and drought have further weakened the natural defences of forests. With the UN's World Meteorological Office predicting the real possibility of a drought next year, the fires could be far worse in future.

John Vidal

- Up to 60 per cent of the fires in Indonesia are the result of arson, according to the EC's Fire Prevention and Control project. This is being taken as an indication of local people's resentment at being denied access to forest resources by logging companies and plantation owners.

Oliver Tickell

John Vidal, 'The nightmare never ends', *BBC Wildlife*, December 1997

Item G7

Seeds of destruction

UK: Genetic pollution threatens organic crops and wild plants.

The widespread use of genetically altered plants in agriculture will make it impossible to maintain unmodified crop varieties and undermine the viability of organic farming, according to Soil Association director Patrick Holden.

The problem, molecular geneticist Michael Antoniou told the International Federation of Organic Agricultural Movements (IFOAM) recently, is that genetically modified (GM) crops can readily cross with other crops and wild plants. In trials in Denmark and Scotland, for example, herbicide-resistance transferred from GM oilseed rape to wild brassicas, creating 'superweeds'.

Likewise, herbicide-resistant hybrid potatoes have appeared in fields as far as a kilometre away from a GM potato crop. 'At the moment, organic food is guaranteed to be genetically intact,' said Holden. 'But, if GM crops are widely deployed ... the chances of maintaining non-GM varieties would be eroded with every passing year.'

Another problem in GM crops is the widespread use of genes from *Bacillus*

Gene blues. Unknowingly, we are probably all eating genetically modified food.

thiringuensis (Bt) soil bacteria, which express insect toxins. Bt cultures are widely used by organic farmers as short-lived natural insecticides which don't create resistance. But the GM plants produce the toxins continually, leading to a rapid build up of Bt-resistant insects. Last summer, in the southern US, farmers growing GM cotton containing Bt toxin genes suffered major losses from boll worms that had apparently developed Bt resistance.

Michael Antoniou warned: 'Once genetic pollution is in our soil, crops, animals and their wild relatives, it cannot be cleaned up or allowed to decay, but will be passed on indefinitely to future generations.'

Organic and consumer groups recently scored a significant victory with the European Commission's decision to label all GM foods. But Holden argues that this is only the beginning of the

campaign. 'Our aim must be to ban GM crops altogether,' he says. 'Such is the groundswell of concern among consumers all over the world that I believe this is a battle we can win.'

Oliver Tickell

- The Hungarian parliament is to debate a law regulating the research and production of GM crops. Close on its heels are the Czech Republic and Poland, also expected to finalise their versions of the laws over the next few months. 'Genetic engineering has been carried out in Hungary for quite a few years, but there was no regulation,' says Dr Mihaly Szanto of the government's environmental protection committee, which approved the draft law. 'We hope that by adopting Western standards we will be secure.'

Sarah Roe (Hungary)

Oliver Tickell, 'Seeds of destruction', *BBC Wildlife*, December 1997

Credit report writing

Report writing on items C1–C3

Using items C1, C2 and C3, write a report on the differing attitudes to preserving biodiversity. You should base your report entirely on the material provided and write about 450 words.

Use the plan below.

- Introduction
- Developments in biodiversity
- The conservationists' point of view
- The oppositional point of view
- Conclusion

Item C1

Eager beavers to return home

Beavers could soon be reintroduced to Scotland's rivers, from which they disappeared more than 300 years ago. But the plan has not been welcomed by all. *Derwent May* investigates.

In a few years, there may be beavers splashing about in Scottish rivers again. They used to be natives of Scotland, but they disappeared from the Highlands more than 300 years ago. Now, the conservationists at Scottish Natural Heritage are thinking about reintroducing them into the wild but are facing stiff opposition from anglers.

Beavers are delightful and on the whole harmless creatures. They do not eat fish though they live among them. In the summer, they feed like gourmets on water lilies and other water flowers; in the winter, they eat the branches and bark of waterside trees such as aspen and birch. They have thick, glossy brown fur and a fat tail like a paddle with which they slap the water as a warning to their family when there is danger. They swim with their webbed hind feet, and they have very sharp teeth.

What they are most famous for is building dams across the rivers they live in. They do this so that the water level will rise behind the dam and create a wide, deep pool.

Meanwhile, on the bank of the river behind the dam, they build a lodge of sticks and mud. The water rises and spreads out all around it, and there they are with a safe home on an island of their own creation. The pool is also useful for keeping large

branches in as a store of food – specially desirable in the winter.

They are very much family creatures. A lodge is usually occupied by a pair of adults, the youngsters from the previous year and in the summer, the newly born young or 'kits' as they are called.

The following year, the older children move off and set up families of their own, and the younger ones take their place.

It is a very well-organised and peaceful life – or at least it was until trappers came on the scene in North America, Europe and Asia. In the 18th century the British and French even fought a war over beavers, so valuable had their pelts become – which broadly speaking, is how we ended up with Canada.

Beavers survive in some of their old haunts on both sides of the Atlantic, but they are always at risk, and Scottish Natural Heritage started thinking about the return of the beaver as a contribution to a European-wide attempt to build up their numbers. It seems as if they could once more become a splendid natural part of the Scottish landscape and ecological system.

For the past two years, studies have been going on into the likely impact of beavers on natural water systems in Scotland, and on the riverside woodlands that they would live

in. Suitable sites for reintroducing them have also been investigated. The best homes for beavers have been found along the rivers of central Scotland – the Ness, Spey, Dee and Don, Angus, Tay and Lomond river systems.

As a very rough estimate, it is thought that these rivers could accommodate 400 to 500 individuals, that is about 100 beaver families.

Last Thursday, Scottish Natural Heritage invited all the interested parties to a meeting in Perth at which it launched a consultation document. It wants to hear what landowners, anglers and anyone else concerned think of the proposal.

Anglers have so far raised the most objections. Among their fears are that trout and salmon may find their movement along a river impeded by beaver dams, that debris introduced into the rivers may do damage, that sediment may spoil the shallow pools where fish spawn, and that access to the flooded riverside for the anglers themselves may become much more difficult.

Scottish Natural Heritage believes, on the contrary, that fish will benefit. Above all, it believes that the rivers will become cleaner, to the great benefit of its fish inhabitants. Sediment will actually diminish, because it will be caught in the

Item C1 (continued)

dams. Acid seeping in from the riverside woodland will not pollute the water but will settle harmlessly in the bottom of the deep beaver pools.

There is evidence that the tiny aquatic invertebrates which fish eat become more numerous when there are beavers in the river, perhaps because of the increased organic matter the beavers introduce. Experience from abroad also shows that trout and salmon have no difficulty in getting through the dams, which are not as impenetrable as they look. The American beaver does indeed build large, formidable dams, but the European beaver – a separate species, and the one that would come back to Scotland – makes comparatively small ones. In times of drought, too, the deep pools will provide a better refuge for fish. Finally, anglers will always get to a river.

Nor is there any serious evidence of harm being done to woodlands. The beavers do, of course, fell trees for their dams, gnawing patiently through the trunk – in fact they can get through a trunk up to a yard in diameter. They also eat bark and sever branches for food. But such assaults on the riverside trees have a negligible effect on the wood behind. The Timber Growers Association is not opposing the return of the beaver.

Certainly, the picture conjured up by Scottish Natural Heritage is a rosy and charming one. We shall be able to see a pair of beavers taking it in turns to chew their way through a tree trunk, while their little kits learn to feed in the pool or the sparkling river. The pool will itself attract more wildlife, such as kingfishers, and when in due course the beavers move and the pool dries out, it will leave behind a rich 'beaver meadow' for wild flowers to colonise. It is like a vision of an ancient Scotland restored. Over the next few years, let us hope it receives the support to become a reality.

The Times Weekend Magazine, 21 March 1998; © Derwent May, The Times, 21 March 1998

Item C2

Pearl fishing outlawed in Scots rivers

Ancient right withdrawn in bid to protect remaining colonies of freshwater mussels

By Graham Ogilvy

A total ban is to be imposed on the ancient Scottish tradition of river pearl fishing.

The Department of the Environment will make the announcement this month, finally ending the right, granted by Royal Charter in 1642, of Scottish commoners to fish for the pearls.

Europe's last significant colonies of freshwater mussels, *Margaritifera margaritifera*, live in Scottish rivers and are already partly protected from amateur fishers.

Scotland is the last country in Europe to allow pearl fishing, albeit under strict conditions, in its rivers. Since 1991, it has been illegal to kill or injure a mussel and next month the first prosecution of a pearl fisher is to take place at Inverness Sheriff Court.

The limited conservation measures have now been deemed a failure and the Wildlife and Countryside Act is to be amended in an attempt to safeguard the future of the species.

Pearl fishers were allowed to continue fishing on the proviso that the mussels – 5% of them contain pearls – were not harmed. Professional pearl fishers, who could earn £4,000 a year, can often tell by the shape of a shell if it contains a pearl and then use special tweezers to remove it without damaging the mussel, which can live for up to 150 years.

It was the allure of river pearls that first attracted the Romans north of the Border ...

... Good specimens can fetch around £350. 'Little Willie', the largest freshwater pearl ever found, discovered in the Tay by Bill Abernethy in 1967, is valued at up to £100,000.

River pearls were once so abundant in the Tay in the 18th century that pearls worth £10,000, a fantastic sum at the time, were sent to London having been gathered in only three weeks.

However, mussels are no longer found in 26 of the 69 Scottish rivers that supported populations. Only the Tay, Spey, and Dee have sizeable colonies. The mussels, which favour fast-running clean waters, have fallen victim to pollution, over-fishing, and also to the mysterious decline in sea trout, which carry mussel larvae in their gills at the earliest stage of development. The demise of the sea trout, which is the subject of scientific investigation, has resulted in fewer young mussels taking root in the river beds.

Mark Young, a senior lecturer in zoology at Aberdeen University, said: 'We have been told to expect the announcement of a ban on pearl fishing within the next two weeks. This is the end of pearl fishing. It is very regrettable, but surveys conducted over the last three years have shown that the plight of the mussels is desperate. We have to have a complete ban, otherwise they will become extinct. There are several rivers in Scotland which only have very old stocks of mussels ....'

... The general manager of Cairncross, the Perth jeweller famed for its use of Scottish pearls, said: 'This could be something of a two-edged sword. Obviously I would welcome a ban if it were an effective total ban. But we would not want to see a contraband trade emerging. Scottish freshwater pearls are popular with our customers. Their beauty, lustre, shape and the fact that they are indigenous make them fabulous.

'But we have noticed that the size of the pearls has reduced in recent years. Perhaps they have not been left long enough to mature. There are many factors in the decline of the pearls and the fishing is just one of those.'

Scotland on Sunday, 1 March 1998

Item C3

Move to save precious river life

Scotland was once famed for its pearls, found in the freshwater mussels which abounded in the clean water of its rivers.

The pearls in the Scottish Crown jewels on display in Edinburgh Castle all came from Scottish rivers, and in recent years the huge Abernethy Pearl was found in a mussel in the River Tay by Scotland's last professional pearl fisher Bill Abernethy.

But now the freshwater mussel and the pearls a very few contain are in danger, thanks to illegal fishing.

Scottish Natural Heritage, with the assistance of police wildlife officers and hopefully the co-operation of salmon fisheries, bailiffs, river gillies and the general public, are trying to prevent a further decline in the population of mussel.

So far scientists have surveyed 69 Scottish rivers known to have held freshwater mussels and only three still have good populations.

Of the remainder 26 have none, nine have only a handful of old mussels which may not be able to reproduce, and 31 have low populations.

SNH scientists estimate there has been a 75% reduction in numbers, mainly due to illegal fishing.

The River Lyon, which once held a good stock, is almost de-populated, the South Esk has had large areas stripped of mussels, and there are not thought to be any left in the River Almond.

Anglers and gillies on the Tay still occasionally find rotting piles of open shells on the bank, the sign that amateurs have been out for mussels.

More professional, but still illegal, pearl fishers tend to hide the shells they kill in opening so their rivals do not learn of the mussel beds.

To try to help the situation Operation Necklace, a clampdown on illegal freshwater pearl fishing, has been announced by police and Scottish Natural Heritage.

Although it is not illegal to fish for mussels and take pearls, it is illegal to kill the mussel.

Operation Necklace will keep a close eye on problem areas, and the public are being urged to help by reporting anything suspicious to their local police station.

A number of landowners are backing the scheme, and estate staff are being mobilised.

At the launch of the new initiative, illegal fishers were warned that under EU legislation they face fines of up to £2000 per mussel harmed or killed – and their chances of finding valuable pearls are remote.

John Ralston, of SNH, said, 'Lots of people are going to be looking out for illegal fishermen.'

Speyside and Tayside are particular targets of Operation Necklace, and in both areas police and SNH staff were out on the riverbanks yesterday looking for signs of illegal activities.

Freshwater mussel expert Fred Woodward said that under the new EU legislation pearl fishing using an aqualung or snorkel is prohibited.

'Only the traditional method – a glass-bottomed bucket and six-foot ash sticks perfected by generations of Scottish pearl fishers, mainly travelling people, is permitted,' he said.

But Fred pointed out that the real professional pearl fishers do not kill the mussel that produces the gem.

The glass bucket and ash pole were used by pearl fisher Bill Abernethy to pick out likely mussels from the river bed, with the result that except in years of very low water, some areas were never fished.

Now, amateurs using aqualungs can reach the deepest parts of the rivers, but many simply break open the mussels, regardless of the size, then discard the dead ones on the shore.

A team of illegal fishers working together can wipe out the mussel population in large stretches of a river.

'It's now totally illegal to take out shells of less than eight centimetres,' Fred said.

He has been campaigning for years to bring in legislation to protect the freshwater mussel and is delighted that it has at last arrived with Britain adopting the EU rules.

The mussel does its bit in improving the quality of water, for it filters out particles from the water to feed on, thus helping the river and the environment, Fred pointed out.

While scientists who in the course of their work need to

Item C3 (continued)

take and occasionally kill mussels must apply for a licence, no fisherman has ever applied to Scottish Natural Heritage licensing officer Mr John Ralston.

Mr Ralston would welcome such applications from legitimate fishermen as their knowledge of mussel populations would be invaluable to scientists.

And another who thinks pearl fishermen should be licensed is Mr Martin Young, general manager of a jewellers whose name is synonymous with Tay pearl jewellery, Cairncross Ltd, of St John's Street, Perth.

Mr Young also suggested that outlets which deal in freshwater pearls should also be licensed.

The freshwater mussel is endangered at world level, declining across Europe, and is a priority under the UK Biodiversity Action Plan.

If anyone should come across illegal pearl fishers at work, Tayside Police wildlife liaison officer Inspector Allan Stewart cautioned, 'We do not want the public to approach these people. Simply report them immediately and leave the police to deal with them.'

He added that it would be helpful, where possible, if car registration numbers were obtained.

Dundee Courier, 18 July 1997; © D.C. Thomson and Co. Limited

Report writing on item C4

Using item C4, write a report on the damage that humans have inflicted on the environment, and the proposed changes.

Base your report entirely on the material provided and write it in no more than 450 words.

Use the plan below.

- Introduction
- The damage to the environment caused by humans
- The proposed changes
- Conclusion

Item C4

SPECIAL FEATURE – BIODIVERSITY – WHAT ON EARTH IS IT?

BIODIVERSITY CONSERVATION – THE CHALLENGE FOR FORESTERS

Biodiversity is a recent addition to our jargon mountain and cynics might be forgiven for thinking that it will be a passing fad. In fact the conservation of biodiversity is now recognised across the world as a fundamental tenet of sustainable use and development of the Earth's resources, including forests which make a major contribution to the world's biological riches. The UK and many other governments have made commitments to sustain biodiversity in international negotiations at, and since, the 1992 Earth Summit at Rio de Janeiro.

Achieving biodiversity conservation in balance with other forestry objectives will be a major challenge for foresters over the decades to come and especially for the next few years. This article aims to describe this challenge from a Forestry Commission perspective and also to update readers with progress since Phil Ratcliffe's contribution in *ICF News* 4/95.

Concepts and objectives

Biodiversity is shorthand for biological diversity: the variety of living organisms and the ecological systems of which they are part. It includes diversity within species (genetic variation), variety of species and variety of ecosystems such as lowland heathland or native pinewoods, which are often called habitats. The varying biological character of landscapes and larger ecological regions is also a part of biodiversity.

The 1992 Convention on Biological Diversity at Rio, which was ratified by the UK, aims to conserve biodiversity at the same time as achieving the sustainable use of its components for this and future generations. Conservation of biodiversity is justified by both utilitarian motives (e.g. economic value from genetic variety and unexploited species and from the suppression of crop

diseases) and moral, aesthetic and spiritual ones (the right to life, cultural values, the human duty of stewardship).

The fundamental aim must be to prevent extinctions and to maintain viable populations of species and areas of ecosystems. Beyond this requirement there is still the need for a large degree of subjective choice to be made by society about how much, where and what sort of wildlife it wants.

Biodiversity conservation can be considered as the next phase of development from 'nature conservation'. The aims are similar but a more systematic and integrated approach is required, which includes all spatial scales (international, national, regional, local, landscape and stand or site), all sectors of society, land-use and business; and all areas, not only designated sites.

The UK Government's Biodiversity Action Plan was published in 1994 and updated with detailed plans for implementation in 1995 (HMSO 1994a, 1995), and has recently been endorsed by the new Government. It gives the overall goal of biodiversity conservation in the UK as:

To conserve and enhance biological diversity within the UK and to contribute to the conservation of global biodiversity through all appropriate mechanisms.

The hierarchy of scales which must be considered is reflected in the objectives, which require the conservation and where practicable the enhancement of:
- the overall populations and natural ranges of native species and the quality and range of wildlife habitats and ecosystems
- internationally important and threatened species, habitats and ecosystems

Item C4 (continued)

- species, habitats and natural and managed ecosystems that are characteristic of local areas
- the biodiveristy of natural and semi-natural habitats where this has been diminished over recent decades.

The internationally important species and ecosystems are mainly those identified in the EU Habitats and Species Directive and the EU Birds Directive.

The UK BAP also stated a set of underlying principles, which included the need for sustainable use of biological resources, recognition of the need for the care and involvement of individuals and communities to achieve biodiversity conservation and a commitment to make biodiversity conservation an integral part of government programmes' policy and action.

The UK BAP approach is to encourage coordinated action between government and other partner organisations by means of action plans for priority species and habitats and for localities or regions (see the article by Clifton Bain).

Biodiversity and forestry

Government policies for conserving biodiversity in forests are set out in *Sustainable Forestry: the UK Programme* (HMSO 1994b). They reflect the broader UK-wide objectives above and identify priority topics such as the diversification of extensive conifer forests, the increase of native woodlands and the conservation of ancient and semi-natural woodland. A key objective is to 'maintain and where appropriate to enhance biodiversity in all our forests and woodlands'. This reflects the legal obligation under the 1985 Wildlife and Countryside (Amendment) Act which requires the Forestry Commissioners to try to achieve a reasonable balance between economic aspects and nature conservation in carrying out their duties under the Forestry Acts. Forestry must of course also comply with the requirements of relevant EU Directives and other UK legislation.

Contributing to biodiversity action plans

The Forestry Commission is developing an approach which aims to contribute actively to the development and implementation throughout Britain of the action plans for threatened species and habitats and local biodiversity action plans. This requires involvement in a considerable number of partnerships and steering groups as well as several coordinating groups at country and UK level. There are opportunities and a need for foresters outside FC also to get involved in local BAPs and the partnerships for habitat and species plans. It will be important to build balanced partnerships of those who manage land alongside those who advocate, advise, develop policies or do the research.

The FC is leading the implementation of native woodland action plans throughout the UK. So far, native pinewoods and upland oakwood Habitat Action Plans have been published. Plans for four more native woodland types are being prepared this year. All of these will set demanding targets for restoration, improvement and expansion of native woodlands over the next 10–15 years. FA national offices will lead the implementation through partnerships of key players in each country, and UK coordination is being developed through a small steering group. On FE land, plans for these key habitats are being prepared to ensure that they are all identified and managed to help meet the national targets. The WGS will be the major mechanism for privately owned woods and FA have introduced WIG projects and Challenge funds to help deliver action plans for both native woodlands and species such as woodland butterflies.

Further targeted incentives and also encouragement of longer-term management plans are being considered. The extent of forestry involvement with species and habitat plans can be indicated by the fact that there will be 24 HAPs and 400 SAPs by 1998. Around 10 and 40 respectively will be of significance to woodland management; many rare species are confined to a handful of sites.

Item C4 (continued)

Local biodiversity action plans are vital for integration of biodiversity conservation with land use and development. FC is engaged in the process to represent forestry interests as a whole. Local landowners and managers also need to be involved to develop a balanced consensus. These plans will not be mandatory but will be used to inform local views about woodland management and expansion and decisions about location of resources by NGOs, local authorities, nature conservation agencies and others. The reconciliation of local and national targets will be needed through discussion and persuasion, since LBAPs are a bottom-up mechanism.

Biodiversity as part of sustainable forestry

The FC is responsible for encouraging biodiversity conservation in balance with other aims of forestry throughout the forests of GB. To do this we need to consider biodiversity everywhere, not just for the key habitats and species with national action plans. We recognise that planted woods of whatever species have a key role to play in conservation and enhancement. This must not be undervalued through focusing only on native woods. We therefore started the Forestry Authority Biodiversity Initiative in 1994 to carry out research and develop guidance. The Biodiversity Research Programme is now in its third year and starting to yield valuable results across a range of issues, including assessment of the current value of planted woodlands for biodiversity and ways of improving it. Although we will not have all the answers by then, FC intends to revise the 1990 Nature Conservation Guidelines in 1998 to give foresters the best current guidance on biodiversity conservation for all woodlands. In the interim, the UK Forestry Standard will contain core information and will be accompanied by a short Guideline Note which will explain biodiversity concepts and key principles.

The challenge for the forestry profession

What will be the main issues for foresters to grapple with? These are some of the key themes emerging, in my view.

- Biodiversity conservation is here to stay. The UK BAP and the international framework to which it contributes provide a great opportunity for foresters to develop a coherent balanced approach to our design and management of forests for nature conservation which integrates with other land uses.
- Partnership working and local involvement to achieve this will be essential; it will also be demanding of foresters' time in the short to medium term.
- We need to develop better definition of agreed biodiversity objectives and priorities in relation to local/regional character and potential and to other objectives of forestry. Although biodiversity needs to be catered for everywhere, targeting our efforts to priorities will be important.
- We must avoid standardised solutions which would reduce diversity at a regional and national scale and stifle creativity, but we need to develop systems of modelling, planning and monitoring which allow us to demonstrate and measure costs and outcomes and improve precision in the future. A particular need is to understand and plan for biodiversity at a variety of spatial scales; modelling, decision support systems and GIS techniques will be key tools to cope with this.
- Foresters need to consider biodiversity conservation as being largely compatible with economic benefits from forests, to promote this concept amongst the public and to adapt forest management systems to achieve it. We must not see biodiversity as a costly add-on to 'normal management'.
- The profession should examine the education and training of foresters to ensure a consistent understanding of biodiversity issues and should contrib-

Item C4 (continued)

ute to education in schools.

- Not least, foresters must help develop understanding amongst the wider community of the choices which must be made between different sorts of wildlife, e.g. red squirrels or oak trees in many regions, so that informed debate about biodiversity issues can take place.

References

- HMSO, *Biodiversity: the UK action plan*, CM 2428, London: HMSO, 1994a
- HMSO, *Sustainable forestry: the UK programme*, CM2429, London: HMSO, 1994b
- HMSO, *Biodiversity: the UK steering group report*, vols 1 and 2, London: HMSO, 1995

BIODIVERSITY CONSERVATION – A PLANNED APPROACH

Biodiversity describes the variety of life on Earth and includes everything from algae to whales. All this wildlife, including ourselves, lives in a delicately balanced environment easily upset by the loss of species and habitats. In the UK alone, over 100 species are thought to have become extinct this century and today many more species and habitats are declining at rapid rates. The challenge for sustainable development is to halt the declines and reverse past losses to our wildlife.

The Earth Summit at Rio in 1992 marked an important stage in the development of a clear strategy for tackling the threats to biodiversity. In response to commitments made at the Convention on Biological Diversity (United Nations, 1992) the UK Government established a plan for biodiversity conservation with clear biological objectives which should guide policy decisions across all areas (HMSO, 1994; 1996).

The UK Government's objective-led approach follows the recommendations of a steering group including representatives from the voluntary sector, academics, industry, land managers and government agencies. The report of this group (HMSO, 1995) lists agreed priority species and habitats based on factors such as rarity, rate of decline, degree of threat and international importance. With limited resources it makes sense to identify our priorities for conserving biodiversity. In this way we can avoid spending effort on less urgent cases at the expense of those elements of biodiversity at greatest risk of loss. From this priorities list, national species and habitat action plans are being prepared which will guide the activities of government departments and their agencies. The plans contain objectives which identify biological ends, for example to maintain the range and numbers of a particular species, and have numerical targets for population size, or area of habitat to be conserved in a given time period. Never before has Government been so clear about what its policies are seeking to achieve for the environment.

It is widely recognised that delivering biodiversity objectives is not just a job for Government; it involves us all. One of the keystones of the planned approach to conserving biodiversity is the need for local action to help deliver the objectives for conserving species and habitats. The mechanism for planning this local action is the Local Biodiversity Action Plan. Local plans follow the same principles as the national plans in terms of setting priorities and objectives. These plans will be largely coordinated by local authorities but there is scope for other organisations to take the lead. Each local plan will bring together key players from landowners, land managers, local industry and academies to local communities in a consensus-building approach which will identify local actions that can be taken to help meet national biodiversity priorities.

The action plan approach is in its infancy yet it is beginning to show considerable benefits. The most striking achievement is that the

Item C4 (continued)

setting of biodiversity priorities and biological objectives provides common goals that a wide range of players can work towards. Addressing the problems facing many species and habitats requires solutions that encompass social and economic issues. The objective-led approach to conservation facilitates positive working among foresters, farmers, government agencies, conservation bodies and local people to help devise practical solutions.

An example of the planned approach can be seen in relation to native pinewoods. This indigenous forest, dominated by self-sown Scots pine, *Pinus sylvestris*, may once have covered over 1.5 million hectares in the Scottish Highlands about 4000 years ago. This habitat is now restricted to some 16,000 hectares. The Native Pine Woodlands Action Plan objectives are to maintain the remnant pinewood areas and restore their natural composition, to expand the current wooded area by 35% over the next 20 years by natural regeneration and to establish new native pinewood by planting or regeneration. Action involves a combination of policy work at local and national government level to support the protection and expansion of native pinewood, advisory work through the statutory agencies to assist land managers and research work to enable monitoring of progress.

An important point to draw out from this plan is that the actions extend far beyond simply undertaking conservation practices in woodland management. If the habitat objectives are to be met, actions need to ensure effective control of deer and support the marketing and utilisation of timber from well-managed pinewoods. There has to be concerted effort involving a broad range of players including the timber processing industry, with Scottish Enterprise providing advice on marketing and utilisation of native pinewoods, as well as those who manage deer, with support from the Deer Commission. Coordinating all this activity at a national level is the role of the habitat

action plan lead player which in this case is the Forestry Commission. At a local level the key players should come together and actions will be coordinated through the local biodiversity action plans.

A similar process can be seen in relation to the key species. Whilst in many cases the actions undertaken towards habitat objectives will secure most of the species needs, care does need to be taken to ensure that the approach towards habitat conservation is securing the species objectives. Take for example the capercaillie which is a priority species with a national action plan already published (HMSO, 1995). Its numbers have dramatically declined in recent decades owing to overgrazing of ground vegetation in its native pinewood habitat along with other factors including collisions with deer fences. The normal approach to restoring native pinewood habitat would involve erecting deer fences to secure regeneration but this action results in the deaths of many capercaillie. The solution to these conflicts lies in taking a more imaginative approach to managing the habitat. The proper control of deer numbers to reduce stocking densities will enable fences to be removed in key areas where capercaillie occur as well as securing habitat improvement.

In conclusion, the conservation and enhancement of biodiversity is a key test of sustainable development and there is much to be done in forestry to address the present declines in biodiversity. A systematic, objective-led approach provides the best means of ensuring that all of us can work in a concerted way to meet the challenge.

References
- United Nations, Convention on biological diversity, New York: United Nations, 1992
- HMSO, *Biodiversity: the UK action plan*, London: HMSO, 1994
- HMSO, *Biodiversity: the UK steering group report*, vols 1 and 2, London:

Item C4 (continued)

HMSO, 1995
- HMSO, *Government response to the UK steering group report on biodiversity*, Cm 3260, London: HMSO, 1996

BUZZ FOR BIODIVERSITY

Baxter Cooper is an ecologist who has worked in the forestry industry for ten years, most recently with Tilhill Economic Forestry. He is now an independent consultant, advising on wildlife matters, carrying out ecological surveys, and producing Environmental Statements for WGS proposals. His number for phone and fax is 01738 860764.

We all know that biodiversity has become a buzz-word, but when it buzzes near me I am inclined to swat it. This is not because it irritates me, but I want to inspect it carefully to see what sort of creature it is. Now, having been asked to contribute some thoughts on biodiversity I have been examining it more closely.

If I am having doubts about what biodiversity really means it is not because I don't support it in principle. It is like motherhood and real ale and I'm all for it. I also welcome the percolation of ideas about biodiversity to the roots of UK Forestry. What makes me uneasy is that the many perceptions of biodiversity are themselves diverse. Much of this is due to the transformation of a credible scientific concern into a village-pump crusade, complete with proclamations, sermons and prescriptions. Just do this or that and win a Brownie point. Forest managers are persuaded to join the crusade, or be conscripted.

Forest managers will have definitions of biodiversity somewhere in the paper pile, and explanations of what biodiversity is all about. In this short article I want to focus on the practical implications of biodiversity by recognising not only what it means but what it does not.

Firstly the conservation of biodiversity is not the same as creating or maintaining wildlife communities. Nailing up a few nest-boxes for blue tits or kestrels will do nothing for biodiversity, and probably planting a patch of broadleaves here or not planting a bog hole there won't either. In the same way prettily strimmed herbaceous borders and a busy menagerie along forest edges are good for wildlife and nice to have, but might contribute nothing to the global need to conserve biodiversity. In fact, provided that nothing of conservation value is lost or threatened, there might be no ecological argument against planting sitka wall-to-wall and by the mile.

Confusion arises from the meaning of diversity. Clocking up a long list of species in a woodland is not a measure of biodiversity, it is merely species-richness. The measure of diversity is in the completeness of natural or semi-natural communities and how scarce these communities, or some of their constituents, are. Scarcity is a matter of context, and whether our woods make a contribution to the conservation of biodiversity is relative.

Foresters do a great deal to enrich our wildlife, and signs of progress are widely evident. Even if few people see it, wildlife has cultural value and it is nice to know it is there. Introducing a variety of habitats induces species-richness, and we grow our woods in a cultural landscape with perhaps more species of wildlife 'fellow-travellers' than the natural landscape ever carried. But forestry is in the business of changing environments, and in a world of rapidly changing environments those species which cannot adapt become extinct. The conservation of biodiversity is about retaining unique species and communities in their natural range, with special concern for those at risk of extinction.

Obviously, of prime concern are those patches of semi-natural habitat which have persisted, including native woodland with associated plant and animal communities.

Item C4 (continued)

Retaining tiny islands or semi-native trees or unplantable bog in a sea of spruce will provide habitat variety and is worthwhile, but small habitats contain fewer species and seldom any rare ones.

Connecting corridors are logical but have still to be proved useful. Scarce species are often scarce because they are poor at moving from place to place.

A new woodland of native broadleaves might quickly become species rich, but because these species are readily available colonists it might not contribute significantly to the conservation of biodiversity for hundreds of years, or maybe never. It is salutary to remember that even rubbish dumps can be species rich.

The need to conserve biodiversity does not imply that every British forest should, or even could, do its bit towards meeting that objective. The conservation of wildlife in general is cared for in the prescriptions for planning and managing under what is termed the New Forestry, and these at least should ensure that scarce species are offered some opportunities to survive. However, biodiversity is a big idea which needs big thinking. Tinkering with forest plans and proposals might not be enough.

So, what can the forest manager do for biodiversity?

- Use the term biodiversity (and even the word diversity) appropriately. Don't confuse it with species-richness and never think that more is better.
- Don't confuse the conservation of biodiversity with more general wildlife conservation objectives.
- Avoid putting rare, scare or diminishing species or communities at risk.
- Recognise relative values. Don't think that a dozen common woodland species can compensate for the loss of a scarce one.
- Question conservation prescriptions but understand and accept valid arguments.
- Retain scarce semi-natural communities and encourage their expansion (however slow that might be).
- Avoid habitat fragmentation and patchy development – think big.
- Don't commit yourself to monitoring ecological change when you mean you will keep an eye on things. Monitoring is another buzz-word, with an expensive sting.
- Above all, remember that scarcity is a relative term, and the value of your woodlands for biodiversity can only be assessed in the context of a much wider role. But if you have concern for wildlife and habitat at your local level then the big idea of biodiversity will be well served.

Institute of Chartered Foresters News; © Institute of Chartered Foresters News, Issue 3/97, 1997

Discursive Writing

Teachers' introduction

Report writing skills require analysing and synthesising the material provided before writing the report. Discursive writing also requires analysis of material, either provided or researched. Pupils could now set up a discursive essay based on the materials provided earlier, the discussions that have taken place, or related material researched from books, the internet or the media.

1.   One way into creative writing is for pupils to explore stories, the idea of myth and the idea of parable. They can then tackle writing a myth or a parable. If they tackle the idea of myth, they can identify a natural form, and through myth tell a story of how it came to be as it is. For example:
    • why is Edinburgh Rock where it is?
    • why are the stars in the sky?
    • why is the grass green?
    • why are there mountains and lochs?

    A local geological feature is obviously ideal for myth making.

    Writing a parable requires that pupils again ignore scientific explanations and write a story to explain geophysical changes in a way that conveys a message or a moral to the reader. For example:

    Our world would be a great deal healthier if people took more care of it.

    Pupils can devise and write a story that conveys this message.

2.   The use of setting, symbolism and personal experience are all very familiar to English teachers. Teachers might choose to use the discussions and preceding reading texts to set up an imaginative piece. This could not be prescribed or suggested in detail in this publication. It would be determined by the pupils' responses to the earlier work.

3.   English teachers are well aware that pieces of creative writing can emerge from material the teacher intended for a different mode, but which pupils have found interesting and wish to pursue. If hijacking the material in this way, by pupils, leads to good writing, increased understanding, and perhaps even a better world, then it has served a good purpose.

The Times Education Supplement Scotland (TESS) printed an article linking environmental education and creative writing. It is reprinted on the next page as an introduction to this section.

Every subject has a part

Fiona Harrison, Glasgow's literacy coordinator, rejects any move to promote literacy at the expense of the rest of the curriculum.

'Environmental studies, for example, is absolutely crucial for children from disadvantaged backgrounds because astonishingly few come with any knowledge of the world, which is essential to inform reading,' Mrs Harrison says. 'The issue is a false dichotomy,' she adds. 'Environmental studies is integral to improving literacy standards.'

Developing reading skills also involves early writing, Mrs Harrison stresses. 'Teachers have to learn that, at the initial stages, they should not be looking for perfectly formed writing but should be encouraging children to have a go. Pupils often have a mental block about completing level A successfully, which prevents them taking risks.'

Have a Go is, appropriately, the name of the scheme Glasgow is now using to promote emergent writing.

Theresa Forsyth, headteacher of Drumry Primary says there are already spin-offs from the emphasis on literacy. Primary 2 pupils are scoring significantly better in maths which requires as much reading as mathematical skill.

Times Educational Supplement Scotland, 27 February 1998

Pupils' notes

Step 1
Decide which area of biodiversity most appeals to you. Set a question in this area for discussion.

Step 2
Research the material you require to provide evidence for your argument. This material may be drawn from the work you have covered, or may be from other sources.

Step 3
Organise this material under headings that will allow you to build your argument – you might find the box plan in the Writing and Solo Talk section (p. 148) helpful.

Step 4
Decide the order of your arguments and how you will link them together.

Step 5
Plan an introduction that draws your reader into the essay and outlines the way that your discussion is structured. Plan a conclusion that brings together your arguments and ties up the essay.

Step 6
Write the essay.